VARIATIONS ON THE
THEME OF MUSIC

VARIATIONS ON THE THEME OF MUSIC

BY

W. J. TURNER

LONDON
WILLIAM HEINEMANN, LTD.

First published 1924

Printed in Great Britain by R. Clay & Sons, Ltd., Bungay, Suffolk

CONTENTS

CONTENTS

vi

I have to thank Mr. Humphrey Milford for permission to include in this book an article on Mozart written for the Oxford University Press.

W. J. T.

MY COUNTRY—THE LAND OF SHAMS!

THE annual Munich Musical Festival takes place at the three principal theatres of Munich, all of which belong to the State. Think of it! Three theatres belonging to the State in Munich and not one theatre belonging to the nation in the whole of England, Scotland and Wales! However, do not let our thoughts linger longer than a moment on this deplorable country. Of these three theatres the oldest, the Residenz, holds six hundred and thirty-seven persons and was built in 1753. It is perhaps the most famous and most beautiful rococo theatre in Europe, and everyone who knows Munich must have a vivid recollection of it. The next oldest, and the largest, is the National Theatre, built in the classic style; it adjoins the Residenz Theatre and is beautifully situated in the principal square in Munich, the Max-Joseph Platz. This theatre was built about 1823 and holds just under two thousand. The most recent of the three theatres is the Prinz-regenten Theatre, which holds about eleven hundred and is built on the model of the Bayreuth Theatre, with a sunken orchestra. The festival

B

performances are divided among these theatres roughly as follows :—The Mozart operas are given in the Residenz Theatre, which is fit and proper, seeing that it was built three years before Mozart was born. It is the correct size for Mozartian opera, and to give any Mozart opera, except perhaps *The Magic Flute*, in a larger theatre is to damn the opera before it begins. The Wagner operas are naturally given in the Prinz-regenten Theatre, which was built for them. It is Wagner's revenge on the citizens of Munich who chased him out of their capital in 1866 from jealousy of King Ludwig's extravagant patronage of the composer. The Bayreuth Theatre was to have been originally at Munich, so the result of Munich's agitation is that the Bavarians to-day have got two Wagner theatres, one at Bayreuth and another at Munich. In Mr. Bruno Walther's office in the National Theatre, Munich, I saw a time-table showing the rehearsals. I saw down for the next day the name of a work that was not to be produced for some weeks to come, and against it this note : "Ninth rehearsal." Just think of it ! Ninth orchestral rehearsal of a choral work that was not to be produced for weeks, but which they would go on rehearsing every week until its performance. Why, an English conductor is lucky if he gets two rehearsals of a new work ! There may be an equal passion for perfection in the souls of some English musicians, but it stands

2

very little chance of surviving the conditions which English musicians are called upon to face. What is the matter with this country artistically is that it completely lacks organisation.

During the Promenade season perhaps twenty thousand Londoners find their way to the Queen's Hall; of those, say five thousand become regular patrons of the various symphony concerts given at the Queen's Hall during the year. But how many of them ever find their way to the chamber concerts, the instrumental or vocal recitals, at the Æolian and Wigmore Halls? I should put the number down as not exceeding a few hundred. A couple of hundred people out of a population of eight millions is all that the unfortunate artist who gives a recital at the Æolian Hall or the Wigmore Hall can count upon! This is no exaggeration, for, after all, those two halls only hold about eight hundred people each, and it is the rarest thing in the world to see either of them full. Not even when a famous quartet is playing—a quartet like the Flonzaley or the Léner Quartet—will you find the hall full. Now, what are we to make of that? Well, in the first place these halls are so small that it would not be worth while anyone giving a single recital in them unless very high prices were charged. Musicians coming to London and counting on giving, say, three recitals in three weeks have got to make enough by those three recitals to pay for the trip to England, a stay

3

here of about a month, with hotel expenses. Well, obviously, if it were not for engagements at private houses it simply could not be done. Therefore these recitals are mostly a polite farce from the business point of view. In fact, they simply serve as an announcement that the artists giving them are now in London and are wanting engagements.

In London's musical life the vast bulk of the well-to-do middle-class London public has absolutely no share. It is Mayfair which goes to the Æolian and the Wigmore Halls, and it is Mayfair that supports all the great artists all over the world; and if it were not for Mayfair, then London would never see the faces of such masters as Casals, Busoni, Cortot, Thibaud, the Capet Quartet, the Flonzaley Quartet, and many others.

Among the hundreds of thousands of Londoners who could afford to pay five shillings occasionally to hear a first-rate musician, there may not be more than a few thousand who could by any conceivable amount of opportunity and education be got to appreciate them; but put the average as low as you will, and yet it must be true that London could do better in support of good music than it does.

Now, is there any way in which this could be brought about? I think there is, but it needs some enterprising concert agent to carry out the idea I have in mind. Supposing a musician

4

coming to London or a native artist were able, instead of giving one or two recitals at the Bond Street or Wigmore Street halls, to count upon at least three recitals a week for three or four weeks in the London area ; suppose, for example, he could give a recital on the Monday at Hampstead, on Tuesday or Wednesday at Hammersmith, on Thursday or Friday at Muswell Hill, and on Saturday afternoon or evening at Forest Gate, and so on, for, say, three weeks. That would mean, say, twelve concerts in three weeks in London alone, which would mean that for each concert he could afford to charge much lower prices. His expenses, in fact, for the twelve concerts would amount to very little more than his present expenses for one. Here, I am sure, lies the way in which the musical life of London may be encouraged. There must be some means of organising a suburban tour. There are plenty of halls lying idle in all parts of London, and it only needs some far-sighted, energetic concert agent to do a little hard spadework for a year or two, and then we should have a first-class suburban circle of halls to which all the famous musicians came just as they come now to the West End.

I don't believe for one moment that the Germans are naturally more musical than we are. I believe that they may have become so through living in a country where artistic activities have been for centuries better organised than ours. Germany owes its present-day artistic wealth—a wealth which has survived the strain of the war and the peace, though this strain has been far greater than that borne by any other country except Russia—it owes this artistic wealth, I maintain, to its constitution, to the fact that it consisted until 1870 of a number of comparatively small States, each with its centre. In short, Germany has never suffered as Great Britain has suffered from the evils of centralisation. Germany does not consist, as England does, of one gigantic, overgrown capital and then swarms of dirty houses and factories gathered into promiscuous and characterless heaps. Leeds, Birmingham, Bradford, Huddersfield, Sheffield, Nottingham, Leicester, Wolverhampton, Northampton, Hanley, Manchester, Liverpool, Glasgow, Cardiff—what are these but a number of featureless smoke and mud pies? Many of them are far larger than Munich, but there is hardly a German town which is not a very paradise compared to them. Industrialism does not ruin German towns as it has ruined English towns, because the Germans had another standard before their eyes. Their petty princes and grand dukes, electors, landgraves, margraves and burgraves had had their town, and in their town their town-residence or palace, and their court and court-theatre, and so formed a nucleus to which could gravitate all the artistic talent of their town or province. In England for centuries all

6

artistic talent has had to gravitate to London, where it has been hard put to not to starve.

A musician to whom I sent the foregoing remarks admitted that it was very hard to exaggerate the superiority of the German town to the English in artistic and intellectual life, but declared that I had accomplished this feat. Well, that is possible; but he went on to say that what I should do to " encourage the woefully low level of art and interest in art in London is not to indulge in this cheap Cockney sneer at the expense of seven-eighths of Great Britain, but to persuade the artist who can do so to return ' into the cave '—or the mud pie—from which he came, so as to spread there the light of metropolitan culture."

Let me say at once that I am not a Cockney, but a provincial. There is no need for me to " repeat ten times nightly, before sleeping, Mr. Desmond MacCarthy's excellent sentences on ' Provincialism,' or to say to myself, ' Provincialism will teach me proportion, perspective and humility.' " As a provincial, these qualities come naturally to me—on the authority of that least provincial of critics, Mr. Desmond MacCarthy. However, like most provincials who possess " proportion, perspective and humility," I have left for London, and I dare not contemplate the present state of my native province. But having arrived in London and surveyed the country, I find no inducement to indulge in

7

" cheap Cockney sneers." What is good in London is the work of the provincials who have collected there, bringing with them their " proportion, perspective and humility." As for the Cockneys, the Londoners, the five or six million inhabitants of Suburbia—well, God help them, for they certainly are incapable of helping themselves !

The self-complacency of Englishmen (or perhaps one should say " Anglo-Saxons "—thus including Americans and the Dominioners) surpasses that of any other race on the globe. No doubt there are in the history of our nation achievements of which any people might be proud, but they belong to the past. The Englishman of to-day is not the Englishman of the sixteenth and seventeenth centuries ; he seems to me definitely inferior, and what virtue remains is the possession of an incredibly small proportion of our population. I believe that the artistic life of a nation is the measure of its real virtue, and if we admit—as I think every informed person will admit—that our artistic life is inferior to that of Germany and France, then we have real cause for heart-burning.

I once went to Brighton to hear the first performance of Mr. Adrian Beecham's opera, *The Merchant of Venice*. I found that the composer had set the text of Shakespeare's play to music. Mr. Adrian Beecham was seventeen years old ; he was the son of a wealthy and dis-

tinguished musical amateur, Sir Thomas Beecham ;
yet there was in his family so little artistic sense
—and by that I mean so little sense of " proportion, perspective and humility "—so little perception, in short—that there was no one to
pull the young composer up and say to him :
How can you think it worth while to give the
public a *substitute* for Shakespeare ? If we ponder
this phenomenon for a moment we shall be
startled by the complete absence of artistic sense
it reveals. For, consider ! *The Merchant of
Venice* is a stage-poem, the work of our acknow-
ledged greatest poet. Does it not contain :

> " The moon shines bright ; in such a night as this,
> When the sweet wind did gently kiss the trees,
> And they did make no noise,—in such a night
> Troilus, methinks, mounted the Trojan walls
> And sighed his soul toward the Grecian tents,
> Where Cressid lay that night.
>
> .   .   .   .
>
> In such a night
> Stood Dido with a willow in her hand
> Upon the wild sea-banks, and waft her love
> To come again to Carthage " ?

Is this poetry or is it nothing—a mere collection
of words ? If it is poetry, then it is complete
in itself. We should no more want to sing the
words than we should want to eat them. The
one idea should be as inconceivable as the other
and, I maintain, *is* as inconceivable to all those
who really perceive the poetry. Our use of

9

words in a non-poetic way for daily business obscures the fact that poetry is an art of words as music is an art of sounds. Poetry is as distinct from words as music is distinct from the bell-clangs of trams, the hootings of motor-cars and the noises of our voices.

Can one imagine anyone who understood music wanting to set a Beethoven Quartet to *words*? The only music that is set to words is bad music —*i.e.* music that is not sufficiently music. Conversely, the only poetry that can be set to music is bad poetry—*i.e.* poetry that is not sufficiently poetry. In this country, where we prefer substitutes to the real thing, we get Beecham-Shakespeare instead of Shakespeare, and Shakespeare-Beecham instead of Beecham, just as we get nut-butter instead of butter and egg-powders instead of eggs.

In no other country in Europe do we get this extraordinary consumption of substitutes. I remember being told by a tea-planter that the best genuine Indian tea is pale and of delicate aroma like the China teas, but that as the English public cannot appreciate this delicate flavour, but has a palate ruined by pickles and preserved meats, and demands something "strong"—inferior tea with stalks and twigs—"rubbish," he called it, is shovelled in and the Englishman gets the nauseating, dark, poisonous fluid which he desires. Where else in Europe but in these islands do we find such a universal consumption of tinned and preserved foods? Londoners have no more palate than they have artistic sense. It is almost impossible to get in London restaurants fresh, unpreserved cream. The public shows as complete an indifference to the fact that 80 or 90 per cent. of our milking cows are infected with tuberculosis as it does to the fact that 90 per cent. of our theatres perform rubbish and 90 per cent. of our newspapers print it. The food in any French or German restaurant, cheap or expensive, will be found far better than in the average restaurant of the equivalent rank in England. This in spite of the fact that Germany, if not France, is a considerably poorer country. What does all this mean? It means simply that our public is less alive, less intelligent, less critical. It is more easily deceived and its reactions are cruder.

The relation between bad food and bad music is a simple and direct one. People fed with inferior food, with cheap substitutes for butter and eggs and with adulterated milk and bread, will have enfeebled and degenerated senses. How can London's millions discern the difference between good and bad music when they cannot discern the difference between good and bad food? It is not a question of money. If the public demanded fresh cream in their popular restaurants, fresh cream would be forthcoming. It costs no more, but the average Londoner simply gulps down what is put before him with complete indiscrimination. It is not owing to popular demand that the standard of the Queen's Hall Promenades is as high as it is. It is kept at that level by Sir Henry Wood and a tiny minority of musicians and critics. You can prove this almost any night by studying the applause given by the audience—and it must be remembered that this audience itself is an extremely select one. It numbers a few thousands among London's millions. Even musicians who ought to know better get corrupted by the public's appetite for impure amalgams and admixtures, an appetite which may be likened to a diseased dog's craving for garbage.

In Munich I once met three young students from the Royal College of Music. Their ability, their enthusiasm and their energy were astonishing; each of them might have had the stuff in him of a real musician, but it was pathetic to hear their ideas as to what they were going to do in England, fresh from the stimulus of the marvels of Munich. They will do nothing, or next to nothing; but it will not be their own fault. The position in England is almost hopeless. There are in Germany a hundred towns with first-rate theatres *in being*, constantly occupied by theatrical companies playing Shakespeare, Shaw, and all the European classics. It is exactly the same with opera. While these towns retain their individuality and flourish as centres of culture, the arts of the theatre and of music will flourish also. They have a corporate life and a strong tradition.

There are only two towns in England that have any conscious corporate life. They are Oxford and Cambridge, and it would hardly be an exaggeration to say that all that is good in England comes from one or other of them, except for those men of individual genius which the English nation keeps on throwing up anywhere in sheer disgust and irritation. Another century, perhaps, and there will be no more of them. God will have given us up.

over and over again—immense vitality and an intellect unusually penetrating and therefore sceptical. If his had been a profound and passionate temperament, such, for example, as Beethoven's, his intellect would have been all to the good; but it is one of the ironies of life that intellect, where it is most valuable, is but rarely present. In Strauss's case we get a combination of sentimentality—which someone has called " the husk of passion "—with great intelligence. This, although less valuable, is a very unusual combination. To realise how sentimental Strauss is, one has only got to listen to his songs, which seem to me to be very slightly superior to the more intelligent Chappell ballads, and superior by virtue of their workmanship (intelligence again !), not of their essential content.

Only an absence of imaginative passion can explain such huge and empty works as *Heldenleben*, with their elaborate ingenuity and expressionless fireworks. Strauss himself was too much of a musician to be satisfied with such orchestral rhetoric and gesticulation. His vitality then drove him into the super-emotionalism of *Salomé* and *Elektra*. Here we get, as in the later tone-poems, a violence of desperation—the violence of a man who, because he cannot find the re-vealing, the illuminating, word, will shout some word that he thinks shocking. *Salomé* and *Elektra* did shock when they were first heard, and it is probable that they would shock again, but who wants to hear, more than once, such Grand Guignol music ? It carries its own death-warrant with it. Yet in spite of these activities, Strauss the musician was not dead, and becoming ever more acutely aware of the lack of specifically musical qualities in his work (as such a Mozart lover could hardly fail to do !), he wrote *Der Rosenkavalier*. Now, here we got unveiled the light-hearted, pleasure-loving, superficially sensuous Southern German, who was disguised from us for thirty years under that huge and elaborate technical apparatus constructed by a first-class brain. A superficial, pleasure-loving temperament, combined with an unusually good head, both for business and for orchestration, gives us a formula which, like all formulas, may be a good deal too simple to cover the real man, but which, nevertheless, expresses, I think, the main truth about him.

Now we can see why Strauss never advanced beyond the work of his artistic boyhood. He had an intellect capable of development, but not a temperament. Ibsen would have said that he was inadequately equipped for suffering. It is one of those æsthetic enigmas which neither Croce nor anyone else has ever explained, that although music is not the expression of emotion, yet the capacity for feeling does vary with the range and depth of the imagination, and that while there is a specifically musical imagination as distinct from a pictorial or a literary imagination, yet that musical imagination varies, not exactly, but in some elusive way in power and range with the personality behind it. It may seem a paradox, but it is a sign of Strauss's deficiency in imaginative power that he should have himself so well in hand, for neither he nor his music bear witness to any capacity for intense and sustained imaginative experience.

If we take him on the sensuous side and compare *Der Rosenkavalier* to Mozart, we have to admit that he shows occasionally—as, for example, in the Rose theme—a sensibility exquisitely exhilarating, a sensibility which Mozart himself would have been the first to applaud. But that fastidious delicacy and clarity which kept Mozart sober even in his most melting moments is not Strauss's. Mozart could be trivial, Mozart could be banal, but when Mozart let himself go, when his genius took his pen, it was a genius of purer fire than the genius of Strauss, who does not seem to have minded which world he belonged to, but has had a leg in both and has finally settled down here. When Mozart, who was never a financial success, related to a friend the particulars of a certain interview he had with the Emperor Joseph, he was blamed for not having seized the occasion " to stipulate for some better provision than you have at present." Mozart, annoyed at this reflection on his want of prudence, replied, " Satan himself would hardly have thought of bargaining at such a moment." Well, Satan might or might not have bargained, but one feels that Strauss would. And, of course, there is no reason at all against it—quite the contrary; but yet that Mozartian simplicity is merely a symptom of a power to forget oneself, a power of complete surrender which is essential to the greatest work.

The performance in December 1923 by Sir Thomas Beecham of Strauss's *Alpine Symphony* was the second in England, Sir Thomas Beecham having been forestalled on November 13th by another conductor. Not since 1914 have musicians in this country shown any real interest in the works of Richard Strauss. The performance of *The Legend of Joseph* in that year was the occasion of a controversy between Mr. Bernard Shaw and Mr. Ernest Newman, but to-day we are far enough from Strauss to find him more boring than Mendelssohn without being far enough to rediscover his merits, while we cannot imagine what Mr. Shaw and Mr. Newman found to dispute about.

I listened carefully to the *Alpine Symphony*— admirably played under Sir Thomas Beecham— and I realised at once that this work, finished in 1915, shows no signs whatever of any decay in Strauss's powers. Those who admired *Ein Heldenleben*, *Also sprach Zarathustra*, and even so early a work as *Tod und Verklärung*, should admire the *Alpine Symphony*, and any pretence that the latter work shows Strauss gone to seed must be abandoned. It is we who have changed, not Strauss, and this points to a radical weakness. Strauss has not developed. As he was thirty years ago so he is to-day. As a man he may have changed his tastes with the rest of the inhabitants of modern Europe, but as an artist he has stood still. I have discussed the reasons for this, but I have not touched upon the question of form, and apart from Strauss's deficiencies as an artist we may now ask ourselves whether his music as a whole does not reveal a weakness which is not his alone, but characteristic of the music of the last thirty years. From one point of view the *Alpine Symphony* may be unfavourably described as a series of coloured views. To declare that its twenty-two sections are like twenty-two coloured picture post-cards of the Alps would be a slight exaggeration. They resemble rather an exhibition of twenty-two oil paintings of Alpine scenery by a brilliant but flashy artist who might or might not have become a Royal Academician. Done into music, however, they seem even cleverer, because the public is not yet quite so well used to pictorial music of such virtuosity. But it is an entirely empty virtuosity. There is no meaning in all this splendour of musical paint. Never once does Strauss express an individual sense of the Alps. There is not a single surprise. We get " sunrise," " ascent," " forest," " waterfall," " apparition " (sun on waterfall), " flowery meadows," " glacier," " summit," " storm " and

" sunset " in all the facile banality of a tourist guide-book. From this music it would seem as if Strauss had only looked at the Alps with the eyes of others. Everything that the average hotel proprietor would put into a prospectus describing the situation of his newly-opened mountain " Grand Hotel Splendide " is set down in clear, unmistakable terms. In music this is undoubtedly an achievement—comparable, shall we say, to a tree carved in marble or the Bernini Daphne and Apollo in the Villa Borghese at Rome. We are glad that it has been done, but chiefly so that no one may ever be tempted to do it again. The history of music of the last thirty years is the history of achievements of this kind. Such is the music truly characteristic of the age. But the structural weakness of Strauss's *Alpine Symphony* cannot be set down to his departure from the symphonic form. We must abandon the old distinction between " absolute " and " programme " music as too superficial, yet it is true that the older composers—of the period from Haydn to Brahms—did consciously always aim first at a formal effectiveness, whereas the modern composers aim first at pictorial or emotional effectiveness. It does not matter whether, like Elgar, they use the old external shapes or, like Strauss, Debussy and Stravinsky, they invent or manipulate new ones. Always their primary interest is not in the structure of their music, but in its emotional or sensuous effect. This explains, I believe, why we have so soon lost interest in the music of Richard Strauss. The fatal weakness of the *Alpine Symphony*, apart from the poor quality of its themes (which reveal the author's comparatively shallow sensibility), is its musical formlessness. Its many brilliant touches are dexterously related and the whole series of musical pictures is ingeniously united in an external framework of twenty-four hours from dawn till night, coinciding with an ascent and descent of the mountains. But this is an imposition from without. It is purely emotional and literary. It satisfies our intelligence, which demands an intellectual coherence of some sort to enable it to grasp the material brought before it. Sensations must have a beginning and an end, or they cease to be apprehensible to the intelligence; but this apprehensible "shape" may vary immensely in significance. It is impossible to conceive of an endless ribbon, but if we take a pair of scissors and cut off a piece at both ends it is immediately an understandable object with which we may or may not be pleased, but that particular "shape" has little if any æsthetic significance. The shape of Strauss's *Alpine Symphony* and the shape of Elgar's *Symphony in A flat* are almost equally devoid of æsthetic significance. They do not satisfy our musical instinct even if they satisfy our logical instinct. Possibly there is no limit to the number of shapes under which the mind of the artist may present itself to us, but some are so deeply fraught with meaning, so inexhaustible in their richness, that we are conscious of being set free. Under their influence we feel and think more profoundly. This magic gesture which frees us is made, I am convinced, in the musical structure of the composition. It is the vital power which gives the work life. Without it no composition, however brilliant, novel, exciting or surprising it may at first sound, can live. I believe it is because composers and musicians everywhere are becoming more conscious of the importance of form that they are revolting against large orchestras and compositions of enormous dimensions. Nothing is less satisfying than noise. Hardly more satisfying are these musical pictures, no matter how vivid. It is not astonishing that in all parts of Europe musicians are writing fugues. But they will not be saved by fugues. A fugue may be correct and yet entirely devoid of musical value, nevertheless to-day a new fugue is a more enticing item on a programme than a new symphony or tone-poem, because it is a sign that form is its composer's chief interest.

NIETZSCHE AND WAGNER[1]

NIETZSCHE we are told in this correspondence first met Wagner at a friend's house in 1868. He was then twenty-four years old and had been an enthusiastic admirer of Wagner's music since the age of sixteen. In 1869, the following year, he was appointed Professor of Classical Philology at Basle and during the Whitsuntide holidays went to Lake Lucerne, where, " finding himself in the immediate vicinity of Villa Tribschen, he debated with himself as to the propriety of accepting Wagner's invitation and paying a call at the villa." While hesitating outside the garden hedge he was observed by a servant, who " came out to say that Herr Wagner was in the habit of working until two o'clock and could not be disturbed before that hour." Whereupon Nietzsche left his card and received an invitation to dinner. This, in the words of his sister, was the " first of those enchanting days with Richard Wagner and Frau Cosima which were to form veritable oases in the desert of his solitary life." " His was not

[1] *The Nietzsche-Wagner Correspondence.* Edited by Elizabeth Foerster-Nietzsche.

the temperament to make friends easily," adds Frau Foerster-Nietzsche, and " he was therefore made indescribably happy by the unexpected cordiality displayed to him by Wagner and Frau Cosima von Bülow, from whom the first advances came."

It must be remembered that at this time Wagner was not married to but was living with the Baroness Cosima von Bülow. Nietzsche was a very young man who had a great dislike of irregular unions. Wagner confided to a friend that his " beloved Nietzsche," who came from a family which could look back on generations of virtuous living, had " suffered unspeakably " over the irregular relations of Wagner's household. Frau Foerster-Nietzsche also tells us that Wagner, " out of consideration for my brother's well-known sentiments and moral scruples, took great pains to conceal from him much that was reprehensible in his own life during the years prior to their friendship." " It has always been my firm conviction," adds Nietzsche's sister, " that it was considerations of this nature which influenced Wagner in relieving my brother from the arduous task of reading the proof-sheets of his autobiography, as he knew that much therein revealed would be offensive to Nietzsche's fastidious tastes. At other times my brother's chastity seemed to irritate Wagner, and he would suddenly break forth into the coarsest and most objectionable expressions concerning himself and Frau Cosima."

It did not take very long for Nietzsche and Wagner to become great friends and, in the autumn of that year, Frau Foerster-Nietzsche tells us that in Wagner's villa " two rooms were set aside for my brother's use, the little salon being christened the *Thinking Room* in his honour." No doubt Wagner welcomed the young professor as an exceptionally gifted and enthusiastic disciple and expected to find him useful. Frau Foerster-Nietzsche says that " neither Wagner nor Frau Cosima had the faintest idea of the demands they made upon my brother's time." Wagner, of course, had had a long life's practice in making use of other people and there is little doubt that *he* knew of the demands he was making.

Cosima, as is the custom with women, took it all for granted, and was probably unaware that Nietzsche was making any sacrifice for the man whom he addressed as " dear and revered master," and who, in return, addressed him as " valued friend."

A valuable friend Nietzsche certainly was. His early writings are full of laudation of Richard Wagner, and his first book, *The Birth of Tragedy*, has a Foreword to Richard Wagner, which is the most magnificent compliment one man has ever received from another : " to be able also to write these introductory remarks with the same contemplative delight, the impress of which, as the petrifaction of good and elevating hours, it bears on every page," writes Nietzsche in this Foreword,

" I form a conception of the moment when you, my highly honoured friend, will receive this essay, how you, say after an evening walk in the winter snow, will behold the unbound Prometheus on the title-page, read my name and be forthwith convinced that, whatever this essay may contain, the author has something earnest and impressive to say, and, moreover, that in all his meditations he communed with you as with one present." Nietzsche then refers to Wagner's " magnificent dissertation on Beethoven," and goes on to say that no doubt many readers " will be shocked at seeing an æsthetic problem taken so seriously," but that " these earnest ones may be informed that I am convinced that art is the highest task and the proper metaphysical activity of life, as it is understood by the man to whom as my sublime protagonist on this path I would now dedicate this essay."

In fairness to Wagner it must be said that he perceived the rare quality of Nietzsche *at once ;* and that, long before the publication of Nietzsche's first book, on reading two of Nietzsche's lectures, Wagner in a letter in this correspondence, dated Tribschen, February 4th, 1870, wrote enthusiastically of the impression made upon him by Nietzsche's ideas, adding :

" At the same time I am deeply concerned about you and from the bottom of my heart I hope that you will not injure your career.

Therefore I should like to advise you not to touch upon such incredible views in dissertations written with the intention of producing an immediate effect, but to concentrate your efforts for a larger and more comprehensive work on this subject, if, as I believe, you are thoroughly convinced of the correctness of these ideas. When that time comes, you will undoubtedly find the right words for the divine errors of Socrates and Plato, both of whom were creative natures of such overwhelming power that, even in turning away from them, we are compelled to worship them.

" Oh friend ! where shall we find adequate words of praise in looking back from *our* world upon these incomparably harmonious natures ? And on the other hand, what high hopes and aspirations we may cherish for ourselves if we realise fully and clearly that we *can* and *must* achieve something that was denied them."

We have got to remember, in reading this letter from Wagner, that it is the letter of a man of fifty-seven years of age to a young man of twenty-six. There are all sorts of hard things to be said about Wagner and, later on, no one was to say harder things than Nietzsche, but that a man after the incredible struggles and privations of such a life as Wagner's, after thirty years of such creative activity as was represented at that date by all his earlier operas, by *Tristan and Isolda*, *The Mastersingers*, and a large part of *The Ring*—that a man should still have the enthusiasm and energy to think of "what we *can* and *must* achieve," as if he were just starting his life, is surely astounding.

Nietzsche's reply to this letter is missing; it is included in that "large number of my brother's letters to Wagner," which Frau Foerster-Nietzsche informs us in her introduction to this correspondence, dated Weimar, October 15th, 1914, "were destroyed in Bayreuth about five years ago, from some reason utterly inexplicable to me." Fortunately, Nietzsche's sister has been able to reproduce a large part of the correspondence from the rough drafts found in her brother's notebooks, but of this particular letter there is no trace.

From this point the correspondence records the history of the friendship which, in spite of Wagner's rather despotic manner of treating his friends, was maintained without a cloud until the year 1873. I have already quoted a part of Nietzsche's dedication of *The Birth of Tragedy* to Wagner; here is the opening paragraph from Wagner's letter, acknowledging the book:

"Dear Friend,—I have never read anything more beautiful than your book! It is simply glorious! I am writing you in great haste, as my excitement is so great at the moment that I must wait the return of reason before being able to read it *carefully*."

It is also worth while quoting a paragraph from Cosima's letter to Nietzsche :

"Oh, how beautiful your book is ! How beautiful and how deep—how deep and how daring ! Did I not feel that you must already have found your highest reward in your conception of things, I would ask, with the deepest concern, where are you to find it ? "

Later on, dated Tribschen, January 10th, 1872, there is a remarkable letter from Wagner, which reveals the instinct with which Wagner's suspicious temperament had realised that Nietzsche was fundamentally independent and that the day might come when he would desert Wagner. The occasion of the letter is simply Nietzsche's declining, on grounds of excess of work, a pressing invitation to visit them at Tribschen. Wagner, says Nietzsche's sister, "construed this to mean that my brother had already regretted having written the work, or, at least, to having had it published." I will quote a few paragraphs from this letter :

"My Friend,—How difficult you make it for me to prove the delight I take in you. . . . From the beginning of our friendship we have observed disquieting symptoms of which it is true you have frequently offered an explanation, but which have then repeated themselves at such regular intervals as to arouse in our minds the most serious misgivings as to the possibility of maintaining our intimate and friendly intercourse.

" You have now given to the world a work which is unequalled. . . . Each of us has read your book twice—once alone during the day, and then aloud during the evening. We fairly fight over the one copy and regret that the promised second one has not yet arrived. I must have it in order to get myself in the proper mood for working after breakfast, as I am hard again at work on the last act since reading your book. . . . For my part I am still somewhat dazed by the thought of having been vouchsafed an experience of this kind. This is the way matters stand with us ! Then we turn to you—and are consumed with anxiety. And just when the most remarkable suspicions have taken hold of us . . . you suddenly break your long silence and inform us that you have been ill.

" These illnesses of yours have already caused us great anxiety, not because they arouse any serious fears as to your physical condition, but rather as to the state of your emotional life. . . . Friend ! what I am now saying to you is of such character that it cannot be put away with a laughing assurance."

I cannot quote this letter further. I have not the space, but it drew what Frau Foerster-Nietzsche describes as "a truly touching reply from my brother," although she does not print Nietzsche's reply, so I presume it is one of those destroyed letters, of which no trace was found in Nietzsche's notebooks.

The next stage in the friendship was Wagner's circular (open) letter in defence of Nietzsche against the attacks of the pedants, Dr. Phil. Ulrich von Willmovirtz-Moellendorff in particular. Then we find Nietzsche taking to Wagner the MS. of his *Greek Philosophy during the Tragic Age*, but Wagner showed his disappointment plainly; he was not, says Nietzsche's sister, "prepared for so remote a subject, but, on the contrary, confidently expected something more directly connected with present problems, with the friends and enemies of Wagner's art and the Bayreuth undertaking. At that time Wagner's every thought and effort were concentrated upon the Bayreuth enterprise, as it was feared that the entire plan was about to suffer shipwreck." Here we are shown Nietzsche in a most favourable light : "keenly disappointed at not finding in Bayreuth, as in the dear old days in Tribschen, the same understanding for his own world of ideas," he nevertheless reproached himself for

" dwelling on the distant heights in the company of Greek philosophers," and upon returning to Basle he " sadly laid aside his *Greek Philosophy during the Tragic Age* and resolved to fulfil Wagner's expectations by devoting himself more to present-day problems." This was early in 1873, and Nietzsche began writing the first of his *Thoughts out of Season*. Later in the year he was commissioned to write an appeal to the German nation for the Bayreuth undertaking to be laid before the delegates assembled in Bayreuth. This appeal, in spite of Wagner and Cosima's energetic support of it, was turned down, as " too serious and pessimistic," by the delegates in favour of an appeal written by Professor Stern. At this " Wagner," says Frau Foerster-Nietzsche, " flew into a terrible rage," and it was only Nietzsche himself who succeeded in pacifying him. The appeal was a failure; it was sent to four thousand book and music dealers towards the close of 1873. " Not a solitary one of these four thousand took the slightest notice of the matter, and only a few thalers were subscribed by some students in Giessen." At that time Wagner was sixty years old.

We now come to the year 1874. Nietzsche learns that the Bayreuth undertaking is on the point of failure and writes to his friend Rohde :

" I have been in a desperate frame of mind since the beginning of the new year, from which I was finally able to rescue myself in a truly remarkable manner. I set to work to investigate the reasons for the failure of the undertaking; this I did in the most cold-blooded manner, and in so doing learned a great deal and arrived at a far better understanding of Wagner than I ever had before."

What this understanding was appears from his notebook of the time. Here is a sentence: " In my student days I said Wagner is a romanticist, not of its art in its zenith, but in its last quarter: soon it will be night! Despite this insight I was a Wagnerite; I knew better, but I could not do otherwise."

The notes in which Nietzsche jots down his reflections reveal an extraordinarily confused state of mind. What Nietzsche believed to be a cold-blooded analysis is really only the expression of a crowd of conflicting sympathies and ideas put down with a sense of drama worthy of Wagner.

This is no defect. A cold-blooded analysis of Wagner's art is impossible, and if possible would be meaningless. As Frau Foerster-Nietzsche says: " There was nothing my brother desired more passionately than to find some being whom he could revere." In fact long before the idea of the superman came to Nietzsche he was instinctively looking for him in the flesh, and he was completely carried away by Wagner, although, as his sister writes : " there must have been times when he unconsciously betrayed his inner doubts and antagonism, and on such occasions Wagner was given to making suspicious remarks." These notes, written about 1874, contain favourable and unfavourable comments on Wagner. They are mild in tone and have little of the brilliance and audacity of that orgy of fireworks which Nietzsche was to write fourteen years later in 1888 in *The Case of Wagner*. Among them there is an interesting tabulation of Wagner's defects, from which I quote numbers

V. Arrogance.
VIII. Friends (arouse fresh suspicions).
IX. Enemies (awaken no respect. No interest in their contentions).

Is it not curious that later on these qualities were to be characteristic of Nietzsche himself ? There are, however, two notes which show exceptional acuteness in an enthusiastic Wagnerite to whom the music was absolutely fresh, for we must remember that at this date (1874) *The Ring* had never been performed and *Götterdämmerung* was only nearing completion.

" Wagner brings together all possible effective elements at a time when popular taste is dulled and demands extremely crass and vigorous methods. Everything is employed—the magnificent, the intoxicating,

35

the bewildering, the grandiose, the frightful, the clamorous, the ecstatic, the neurotic. Prodigious dimensions, prodigious resources.

"Wagner has a dictatorial nature. He overlooks many minor circumstances and does not occupy himself with small matters, but disposes of things 'in a grand style.' Therefore he is not to be judged by isolated details—such as music, drama, poesy, the state, art, etc. The music is not of much value, likewise the poetry, and the drama even less."

"While my brother was unburdening his heart after this fashion," says Frau Foerster-Nietzsche, "he suffered intensely from the fear that Wagner would never be able to carry out his plans." In fact Nietzsche's criticism was as yet merely the recognition of imperfections in his idol. It is a great pity that Wagner's Autobiography stops at the year 1864, otherwise we might have had Wagner's account of the imperfections of his friend Nietzsche. A certain Privy Councillor Ritschl had once said (rather unfairly when we consider all that Nietzsche had done for the Bayreuth scheme) that Nietzsche was of no use in party factions, but this only testified to Nietzsche's rare quality of intellectual independence, which was more fully realised in Wagner's own comment: "Nietzsche always goes his own way, and one has to take him as he is." This is a better remark than Nietzsche's : "Wagner has a dictatorial nature."

In February, 1874, Nietzsche sent Wagner his second *Thoughts out of Season*, namely, the essay on "The Use and Abuse of History." It is a wonderful essay. Extraordinarily penetrating, learned and brilliant. One reads it with astonished respect and with constant amusement. It is full of sallies like the following :

> "If you try to further the progress of science as quickly as possible, you will end by destroying it as quickly as possible ; just as the hen is worn out which you force to lay too many eggs. The progress of science has been amazingly rapid in the last decade ; but consider the savants, those exhausted hens. They are certainly not 'harmonious' natures ; they can merely cackle more than before, because they lay eggs oftener ; but the eggs are always smaller though their books are bigger."

Now this early essay of Nietzsche's is not fairly represented by such a quotation. It is an essay full of hard thinking, but it is entirely without coherence. An hour after reading it one is completely unable to give a summary of it. The essay has no meaning, but only a mass of meanings. What does this imply ? It implies that it has no artistic form. Yet it is full of ideas of a quality far beyond the power of Wagner to conceive.

As far as I can see, however, these ideas, scattered thus promiscuously, and half embedded in their context, have no value. I don't suppose anyone reads *The Use and Abuse of History*; certainly, I shall never read it again, but I shall often hear *The Ring* and *The Mastersingers* again; so it seems to me that the advantage so far lies with Wagner, who on receipt of this essay wrote to Nietzsche : " Eight days ago we received your new work from the book-dealer and have deliberately devoted three evenings to the reading of the same." I may be a very self-centred character, but it amazes me that Wagner at sixty-one should devote three evenings to tackling *The Use and Abuse of History*. Here is a further extract from Wagner's letter :

> " You certainly do not expect praise from me ! It would be a fine thing, indeed, for me to presume to praise *your* wit and *your* fire. My wife always finds just the right tone for anything of that sort, for else why should she be a woman ? She will not fail to let you hear from her on the subject.
>
> " Now may God bless us all together ! Nor will He have a very big task, as there are so few of us."

And now comes an incident which reveals to us how far Wagner fell short of Nietzsche's ideal of a great artist. In the spring of 1874 Nietzsche heard a performance of Brahms' *Song of Triumph*

38

in Basle Minster and, much impressed by it, he bought the score and in the following August took it with him to Bayreuth. He wished to make an effort to induce Wagner to be just and generous towards Brahms. But it was the cause of an extremely painful scene of which Nietzsche said nothing, but Wagner himself " related it to me," says Frau Foerster-Nietzsche, " some months later in the rare way he had of speaking ironically of himself : ' Your brother laid the red-bound book on the piano, so that my eye fell upon it every time I came into the room and enraged me as a red rag does a bull. I knew perfectly well that Nietzsche wished to say to me : " See here ! Here is someone else who can also compose something worth while ! " I stood it as long as I could, and then one evening I let go of myself, and how I did rage ! ' Wagner," adds Frau Foerster-Nietzsche, " laughed heartily as he recalled this scene. ' What did my brother say ? ' I asked anxiously. ' Not a word,' was Wagner's reply, ' he grew red in the face and stared at me with a look of astonished dignity. I would give a hundred thousand marks all at once if I were as well-bred as Nietzsche ; he is always the aristocrat, always dignified. Such deportment is of the utmost value to anyone.' When I later questioned my brother about it, he was silent for a moment and then said softly : ' Lisbeth, at that moment Wagner was not great.' "

I cannot read of this incident without the phrase "the lonely Nietzsche" coming to my mind. Does not one feel compassion for this man tormented by a raging thirst for perfection, a perfection for which his hero, his superman, his idol, has no use and which he would think ridiculous?

Nietzsche considered that Wagner's reception of *The Use and Abuse of History* was chilly. Frau Foerster-Nietzsche says: "Wagner's indifference and adverse criticism of the second *Thoughts out of Season* had a depressing effect upon my brother at Easter, 1874; it was then that he said to himself with a heavy heart: 'It has become plain that my only value lies in being a Wagner commentator: I am to be nothing more. I am permitted to admire only *that* which is stamped with the seal of Bayreuth's approval.'" On October 10th, 1874, Nietzsche sends Wagner a copy of his third *Thoughts out of Season*, entitled "Schopenhauer as Educator." He receives the following telegram:

"Deep and great. Presentation of Kant boldest and most original idea. Verily, only intelligible for those who are possessed. I can picture to myself the three just men. May they cast long shadows in the sunland of the present.—Yours, R. W."

I am quoting from an American translation, nevertheless I think one would also get from the original of this telegram an impression of charlatanism. But let us remember that saying of Stendhal : " Charlatanism *added to genius* is like a nought added to a figure, it multiplies it by ten." What, after all, is charlatanism in this connection ? Is it anything but sheer, flashing, instinctive exuberance ? There is little doubt that Wagner never understood Kant, possibly he had never even read him, but he had read, understood and absorbed a great part of Schopenhauer. Schopenhauer had been a genuine influence in his life, and Wagner had genius, he had that intense exuberance which is the hall-mark of genius and he could understand instinctively what Nietzsche was driving at in this essay, for it was not such a piece of critical ratiocination as the *Use and Abuse of History ;* it was rather a pæan in honour of great men, a magnificent " call " to men to *be* great and, in Nietzsche's later phrase, " to live dangerously."

Therefore we must not laugh at Wagner's telegram or have only the cheap notion that Wagner delighted in " Schopenhauer as Educator" simply because in it he was named with Schopenhauer as a leader of men. Yet, in a letter of Nietzsche's at this period occurs the following sentence : " A cloud of melancholy settles on our brow, for the thought that speciousness is a necessity is as hateful to us as that of death itself." But if Nietzsche resented any speciousness in Wagner, it was also because of its producing so much in himself, for his sister writes : " I should not like to state positively that my brother expressed himself as candidly in his letters to his Bayreuth friends. There were several reasons for this, one of them being his desire to avoid anything that could possibly give offence to his dearly-beloved friend, and furthermore his regard for the formalities of polite intercourse." Nietzsche combined with an intellect of extra-ordinary power and acuteness a quite abnormal sensitiveness, and therefore his friendship with Wagner, whose irrepressible buoyancy of tempera-ment must have frequently jarred on him, was a continual strain. They were both men of astonishing exuberance, but Wagner was genial while Nietzsche was misanthropic. Nietzsche had a passion for abstract, unattainable perfection, Wagner for beautiful women.

As the essence of Nietzsche's teaching may be given in the phrase, " be discontented," the genius of a man who had never known real dis-content was his principal enemy. Nietzsche becomes slowly conscious of this, but he is still under the spell of his old love and admiration for Wagner when, in 1875, being unable through illness to go to Bayreuth, he begins, but soon lays aside, his fourth *Thoughts out of Season*, " Richard Wagner in Bayreuth." Early in 1876 came the news that the long-anticipated Festival was at last to be held that year in Bayreuth. " Gratitude for all the blissful hours and the untold inspiration that Wagner had brought into his life impelled him to resume work on his " Richard Wagner in Bayreuth." On the occasion of Wagner's birthday he writes him a moving letter dated Basle, May 21st, 1876, beginning " Deeply revered man." This letter must be looked up in the correspondence, I cannot quote it here. In July it was followed by a letter enclosing his fourth *Thoughts out of Season*, " Richard Wagner in Bayreuth." He received immediately the following note :

> " Friend,—Your book is simply tremendous ! Where did you learn so much about me ? Come to us soon and accustom yourself to the impressions by attending the rehearsals.—Yours, R. W."

I find a note of extreme sanity in this Olympian rhetoric of Wagner's. In a man of whose greatness we had no proof such Horatio Bottomley rodomontade would be laughable ; in Wagner it is tremendous, almost terrifying. It shows Wagner's power of self-preservation. He kept everyone, including Nietzsche, at arm's length— not consciously but instinctively—and he did it like he did everything, with gusto.

In the summer of 1876, at the age of thirty-two, Nietzsche goes to the opening Bayreuth Festival ; he has just declared in his latest work : " Bayreuth signifies to us the morning sacrament on the day of battle." Of the original gathering in 1872, when the foundation-stone was laid, he had written : " In Bayreuth the spectators themselves are worthy of being seen." At this earlier event the participants, writes Frau Foerster-Nietzsche, " were all invited guests known to Wagner and his co-workers as persons of like ideals and aspirations. . . . In 1876 anyone able to pay the sum of 900 marks for the twelve performances was free to come." What was the new type ? It has been set down once for all in the famous drawing by Aubrey Beardsley. In 1876 bloomed together from all parts of Europe those gross, sensual, over-fed mountains of flesh, the Wagnerians. They had found a new social pleasure. " It seemed," writes Frau Foerster-Nietzsche, " as if the entire leisure rabble of Europe had met here." *What was it that had attracted them ?* Nietzsche " wandered around like a man in a dream." The deed was accomplished, the word was made flesh. " Wrapped in that deep Pythagorean silence to which he had admonished his readers," Nietzsche suffered the disillusionment of all idealists. One discerning woman said to his sister : " Why does your brother avoid all mention of his last work ? " When this was repeated to Nietzsche he exclaimed : " Why cannot people let these old stories rest ? " " To which remark," says Frau Foerster-Nietzsche, " I gave the astonished answer, ' But, Fritz, the work only appeared five weeks ago.' ' It seems five years to me,' was his only reply." During the Festival Wagner seemed eager to single

Nietzsche out and do honour to him on all occasions. "My brother endeavoured to ward off these noisy demonstrations, as Wagner's boisterous praise was extremely distasteful to him. Moreover, both of them felt that something unexpressed lay between them, and there were none of those deep and great moments which might have bound my brother anew to Wagner. Was not such a moment once near? I remember quite well that we walked out to Wahnfried one morning, and met the master in the garden, on the point of going out. I cannot recall just what Wagner said, but I remember that my brother's eyes suddenly lighted up and he fairly hung on the master's words with an expression of the most tense expectation. Did he think that Wagner would say, 'Oh, friend, the entire Festival is nothing more than a farce! It is not in the least what we both have dreamed for and longed for?'" But this hope was soon dispelled. "The light died out of my brother's eyes as he saw and felt that Wagner was no longer young enough to take sides against himself." Before the Festival was over Nietzsche left. "'Ah, Lisbeth, and *that* was Bayreuth!' he said to me as he bade me good-bye. His eyes were filled with tears."

Of the history of the actual break something, but not all, may be learned in this correspondence. Nietzsche went his way to do the work which awaited him and which no one else could do. Years later, in 1882, his sister went to the Festival.

It was six months before Wagner's death. After the performance of *Parsifal* Wagner asked to see her alone. " ' Tell your brother,' he said softly to me, ' that I am quite alone since he went away and left me.' " On hearing this touching message Nietzsche wrote in his notebook : " We were friends and have become as strangers. . . . Let us *have faith* in our stellar friendship even though doomed to be enemies here on earth."

SUNDAY MUSIC

THE National Sunday League was established in England many years ago, about the middle of the dark ages—I am not referring to the tenth or eleventh century, but to the nineteenth, that era when the youth of Great Britain groaned under a puritanical tyranny worse than anything ever devised by the most barbarous of Asiatic despots. It was started so far back as 1855, and such was the spirit of the times that its objects were defined in the humblest, psalm-singing phraseology so as not to give offence to the worthy gentlemen who from Monday to Saturday swindled their fellow human beings, sweated their employees, grew rich on child labour and on Sundays took round the plate and described their mistresses as whores of Babylon—for they often had mistresses, these hard-faced Puritans, generally some wretched, underpaid servant or employee whom they cowed and bullied! But such then was the general cowardice, the fear of being thought immoral or not respectable, that nearly everybody—and certainly everybody in public life, dependent on popular favour—paid lip-service to these " religious " pretensions which cloaked alike the knave, the hypocrite and the mere fool. So the founders of the National Sunday League, timid as they may seem to us to-day, were really exceedingly bold when they went the length of starting a League to promote the Sunday opening of museums, art galleries and libraries, the running of Sunday excursions, and the playing of Sunday bands in the parks.

There are still places in this country where people are not allowed to play tennis on Sunday —public courts and private courts ! But the opponents of Sunday sports are beginning to feel conscious that they look uncomfortably silly. Nowhere, however, does there appear to linger any opposition to " secular music." " Secular music " was one of the greatest inventions of the perverted wit of mankind, alias the devil ! Our grandfathers would have fainted or have had a fit if anyone had sung or suggested singing an operatic aria in their presence on a Sunday, but looking at the programmes of the National Sunday League's vast organisation, I find that operatic music figures very largely in them, so that we may conclude that " sacred " music is, for the time being, dead. I say " for the time being," because the type of music which was called " sacred " during the nineteenth century was quite arbitrarily chosen for that honour. England being then at an extremely low stage of æsthetic perceptiveness, even those who could boast of what education there was, were unaware that there was such a thing as musical virtue as distinct from moral virtue. Having painfully made that distinction clear to ourselves, we have begun to perceive that it is extremely doubtful whether the words " moral virtue " mean anything at all.

I shall say nothing further on that subject, but regarding " musical virtue "—which is something much more concrete—it is quite clear to me that there is, absolutely, no such thing. Any standard we like to set up will be relative. No one can say of any music that this is absolutely and eternally the best; the utmost that he can say is that it is the best so far, and even this has to be qualified to the admission that others may think differently.

Our grandfathers called that music " sacred " which they genuinely thought to be the best. They judged music by its associations. If it contained references to God, apparently polite; if they heard it in church or at church concerts; if it was set to words of unimpeachable piety, it was " sacred."

Finally, by a strictly logical process, all that became necessary to distinguish music suitable for the Lord's Day from music suitable to the six days belonging to the devil was that the publishers should mark the Lord's music " Sacred " on the cover or wrapper. Obviously, some such method of distinction was necessary, since no

E

man could be expected to remember where he had first heard any piece of music—whether at church, chapel or night-club—nor could one be sure of always hearing and understanding the words—witness the words of comic songs that used to be sung undetected to ecclesiastical music in the Sistine Chapel!

But do not let us laugh too loudly or too long at the follies of our grandparents. Is it possible that *we* do not deceive ourselves at all? No, it is not possible; and I suggest, with due respect to Mr. Edwin Evans, Mr. Eugene Goossens and Mr. Arthur Bliss, that what our grandfathers did with the word " sacred " we, to-day, do with the word " modern." The methods by which man hoodwinks himself are infinite, and it is just as unsafe in certain circles to-day to perform the music of Brahms and Schumann, Max Reger and Strauss, Verdi and Wagner, as it used to be to sing Gounod's *Faust* on a Sunday. Therefore, I am not so perturbed as some of my friends are at the popular character of the programmes of the National Sunday League concerts, but I do share the alarm at the tendency to turn these concerts into mere assemblages of indifferent vocalists of the ballad-singing variety, and music-hall turns of a concertina and rag-time type. One of the main objects of the founders of the National Sunday League was to promote—I use their own words—" intellectual and elevating recreation on that day." Well, although that phraseology sounds almost absurd, because we have come to recognise how narrow are its implications, yet it does serve as a declaration that the objects of the National Sunday League are not primarily commercial. Yet I am afraid that the League has every appearance to-day of being purely commercial. In and around London it controls, every Sunday, concerts at the Palladium, the Holborn Empire, the New Islington Empire, Finsbury Park Empire, Alexandra Theatre, Stoke Newington, Chelsea Palace, Hammersmith Palace, the Grand Palace, Clapham Junction, Kilburn Empire, Woolwich Hippodrome, Camberwell Palace, Empress Theatre, Brixton, Lewisham Hippodrome, Croydon Empire, Richmond Hippodrome, Stratford Empire, East Ham Palace, Bedford Palace, People's Palace, New Cross Empire, Watford Palace, and the Southend Hippodrome.

Thus the influence of the National Sunday League on the musical tastes of the population of London is incalculable—far greater than that exercised by Sir Henry Wood and his Promenade Concerts ; but so far as I can see, it is exercised entirely without control by the secretary, Mr. Henry Mills, and there is no evidence that any attempt is being made to raise the standard of taste at all. There is a huge demand for recreation on Sundays in London, and the National Sunday League is just catering for that demand as any purely commercial firm of caterers might do. This was surely not the intention of its founders. The National Sunday League must make a steady, persistent effort to raise the musical standard of its public or it fails to justify its existence. I believe it has a board of trustees or guardians, of whom I believe the Earl of Plymouth is or used to be a member. I should like to draw the attention of the members of this board to the urgent necessity of associating with Mr. Henry Mills, as an advisory colleague, a musician of standing with broad and catholic sympathies, whose business it would be to introduce a leaven of better music and of better artists into the League's operations. How this should be done is a matter for discussion, but one thing is clear, it is useless to attempt isolated improvements. What is wanted is the engagement of a good orchestra under some first-class musician like Mr. Adrian Boult to give regular concerts. The assistance of Mr. Cecil Sharp and the English Folk Dance Society and of the Oriana Madrigal Society should also be sought. With the co-operation of some of these societies and some of our younger musicians, the National Sunday League could do more for music and for the public in five years than has been done during the last century, and earn that respect for its work which it lacks utterly at present.

THE PERFECT FOOL

TO anyone familiar with musical history this phrase, "The Perfect Fool," will immediately suggest Wagner. Has that anything to do with Mr. Gustav Holst's choice of the title of his one-act opera? Produced at Covent Garden, this "opera" aroused a good deal of curiosity, for Mr. Holst is well known as one of the most skilful of contemporary English composers.

No doubt Parsifal was not a perfect fool, however desperately Wagner may have attempted to make him one. There is a good imitation of rationality in Parsifal; his actions are comprehensible, even sane. His resistance to the wiles of Kundry and the Flower-maidens may not seem to have been determined by ordinary motives of self-preservation, but the result was the same. Dostoievsky also tried to conceive a perfect idiot, and to an English translation of the book in which he made this brave attempt, the title of *The Idiot* has been given. But Dostoievsky tells us in a letter to A. N. Maikov that his idea was " to depict a *thoroughly good man*," and he adds: " In my opinion there can be nothing

more difficult than this, above all in our time."
Modern Germans have made numerous attempts
to create Fools or Idiots. They have mostly
taken the historical figure of Jesus for their
model. If I remember rightly, in one German
work which expressed this great ambition, the
hero Fool is sent to America in an Atlantic liner
which splits and founders under his inspired
weight.

All these " Fools " and " Idiots " are comprehensible enough. The common sense of mankind readily recognises the need for other standards
and ideals than its pedestrian own. In fact, the
world welcomes Fools with a quite peculiar
ardour, relieving them of their reputation (a
necessary preliminary), their money and their
liberty, encouraging them to attain to the utter-
most heights in stark nakedness of folly.

But Mr. Holst's " Fool " does not appear to
be a Fool of this sort. He has none of that
sublimity which encourages the wise to remove
from the Fool all the material impedimenta which
enwrap, cloud and obscure sublimity from his
sight. He seems to be merely one of those
unfortunate creatures usually described as con-
genital idiots. But perhaps at this point I had
better give an outline of Mr. Holst's " drama,"
which even more than the music is " all his
own." The curtain goes up on a scene which
suggests witchcraft. A big piece of Stonehenge
is suspended over a well. On the well is a silver

chalice which might serve equally for *Parsifal*
or a Communion service. A large Wizard " is
performing a magic rite." He summons spirits
of earth and water, who dance before him.
Upon this scene enters a Mother, dragging her
son, the Fool, whom she describes thus :

> " He wins a bride with a glance of his eye :
> With a look he kills a foe.
> He achieves where others fail—with one word."

Unfortunately, she adds, he never opens his eyes
and he never speaks. He seems to have been
born blind, deaf and dumb. Well here, no
doubt, we have the Perfect Fool at last. There
may be qualities which he does not lack, but
they are—after those preliminary disadvantages
—almost negligible. So we see that Mr. Holst's
" Perfect Fool " is quite unlike all the other
" Fools " of art. He is arrived at by an easy
process of subtraction. He is not a " created "
Fool, he is a minus Fool : Man — sight — hearing —
speech = Fool. Nearly all the fools we meet
with are more subtle than that.

The Wizard now catches sight of the Mother
and utters a fearful curse.

> " Cursed be the man who hears my voice or sees me !
> His ears shall wither, his eyes be burnt to ashes,
> His mouth be filled with scorpions,
> His hair be turned to flames of fire—
> His nose——"

He is interrupted by the Mother, who points

out that she is a woman. The Wizard admits that his curse only applies to men, but, like most stage wizards, his wizardry is partial and at the mercy of those ordinary senses which he shares with other men. He fails to perceive the presence of the Fool, and proceeds to show Mother the magic potion and to explain exactly to her how valuable it is :

> " In taste and colour
> It is pure as water ;
> If a woman drink
> It is but water.
> If a man drink,
> His eye is all-powerful."

In short, it will cause the first woman he looks at to be filled with " love-longing " for him, and if he looks at a man flames of fire will rise from the ground and burn him—which is perhaps the most sensible meaning of " all powerful " ! After giving away this valuable secret from sheer wizardic boastfulness he goes on to say that he has not drunk the potion, but will do so when he sees the Princess.

The Wizard now goes to sleep in order that the Fool may drink the potion which his Mother pours down his throat, replacing the liquid with water. Then the Princess arrives, the Wizard awakes, drinks the water, harangues the Princess and fails lamentably. One cannot help feeling that Mr. Holst had *Tristan and Isolda* in mind when he first conceived this potion business, but it is not a parody or a burlesque or in the slightest degree a criticism of Wagner's drama. It produces on the auditor indeed the impression of complete pointlessness.

After the exit of the Wizard, breathing curses, appears a Troubadour who woos the lady in the best Italian operatic style. This " parody " of Italian opera is the sort of thing that any intelligent student could write. The Troubadour is followed by a Wanderer (Wotan, obviously) who hails the Princess with an outburst of Wagnerian music. He retires rejected, falling over the Fool, who looks up straight at the Princess, and the potion works. The Princess is enraptured.

The " opera " concludes with the return of the Wizard and his spirits of fire, whom the Fool vanquishes with a glance. The Princess then asks the Fool if he loves her and he utters his first and only word, " No ! " Whereupon his Mother cries : " He has achieved where others failed, with one word." A Priest appears, puts a crown upon the Fool and the curtain falls.

The Princess may represent the public, the Fool may represent the Cinema—which is dumb and blind and perhaps utterly silly, but which has won the applause of the masses as Drama and Opera (Italian or Wagnerian) have not done. But, on the other hand, it is not by its pure folly that the Cinema has become popular, but merely by its comparative cheapness ; so if that is the point of the satire or allegory it is a blunt one. In a note the author asks " that the spirit of high comedy shall be maintained throughout." It is as if an author were to request the actors in a dull play to preserve its humour. It is impossible to maintain a spirit of high comedy when there is no high comedy, and I can find none in *The Perfect Fool*.

Musically, Mr. Holst's work is a *pastiche*, but it is not an amusing *pastiche*. The opening Ballet is lively, but reminiscent of Saint-Saëns in its commonplace Oriental colouring. The burlesques of Wagner are dull. The one bright touch is the trio of water-carriers, which is lyrical and has a certain distinction, but one bright moment does not make an opera—even an opera in one act that only lasts an hour and a half.

AN ELIZABETHAN PLAY WITH MUSIC

I MUST confess that when the curtain went up on *The Faithful Shepherdess* I thought I was in Paradise. It is true that I had been beguiled by an overture conducted by Sir Thomas Beecham which I could not identify, but which had a certain flavour of Rameau, but this—even played with that virtuosity one has learnt to expect from Sir Thomas Beecham—was not of itself sufficient to enfold and spirit me away into Arcadia. But it had prepared me, and when the curtain rose upon the bower of that holy Shepherdess Clorin—a bower of the most apt, ingenious and artificial naturalness—and I heard these first words of Clorin, beautifully spoken by Miss Nell Carter :

> " Hail, holy earth, whose cold arms do embrace
> The truest man that ever fed his flocks,
> By the fat plains of fruitful Thessaly,"

I was enchanted. Sir Thomas Beecham had contrived an accompaniment to Clorin's blank verse which did not disturb or cloud one single syllable from her lips, but which provided a rhythmic background over which the blank verse rhythm moved freely with an accentuated music. I had not thought it possible so to enhance the beauty of the spoken verse, and the whole credit of this achievement, which was sustained throughout the play, is due to Sir Thomas Beecham, who could thus choose the appropriate music, and control tone and rhythm with such flexibility that the verse not only retained its rightful prominence but, as it were, floated upon the music like a boat, silhouetted upon flowing water, that moves in harmony with with the wind and waves.

Much of the initial effect must also be credited to Mr. Norman Wilkinson of Four Oaks, whose dresses and scenery were exquisite in colour and design. This production is, perhaps, the best thing he has ever done, and it demonstrated vividly how great a loss the theatre suffers by the continued unemployment of such proved artists as Mr. Albert Rutherston and Mr. Norman Wilkinson himself. It is years since there has been seen upon any London stage scenes which gave such delight and satisfaction to the eye. Perhaps the most striking of Mr. Wilkinson's successes was the well scene, where one expected to see arise Sabrina fair :

> " Under the glassy, cool, translucent wave,
>   In twisted braids of lilies knitting
>   The loose train of thy amber-dropping hair,"

but, as the author of the piece was John Fletcher and not John Milton, actually there arose from

the well at his appointed time in the play, instead
of Sabrina, the God of the River, and in the finest
invented silver-watery dress I have ever set eyes on.
Many were the successful dramatic musical touches
contrived, I suspect, by Sir Thomas Beecham
himself, and woven into the actual musical
material which he had collected—if my ear
judges correctly—from various minor eighteenth-
century works plundered for his purpose; but
there was one seeming interpolation which I did
not think successful, namely, the song of the God
of the River, beginning :

> " Do not fear to put thy feet
> Naked in the river sweet."

This song was distinctly poor and also, I thought,
struck a false note. Mr. Frederick Ranalow, who
took the part, did not succeed in hiding its defects.
I imagine that many people would also dislike
the rather sing-song way in which he delivered
his preceding lines, written in couplets; for,
compared with the vocal resource in diction of
Miss Nell Carter (Clorin), Miss Isabel Jeans (Cloe)
and Miss Cathleen Nesbitt (Amarillis), Mr.
Ranalow's capacity to speak verse was decidedly
limited. But I thought this sing-song effect
rather in place, being curiously appropriate by
contrast with the subtler speech of the mortals.
It provided one of those examples of happy
accidental effects which occasionally reward pro-
ducers, since Mr. Ranalow had obviously been

cast for the part of the God of the River because of the song to be sung. The song was a failure, but his first appearance and opening speech were surprisingly successful.

The Faithful Shepherdess, published before 1610, is the work of John Fletcher alone. One cannot but regret that Francis Beaumont did not collaborate with Fletcher in this play, for he might have lopped off a few extravagances, condensed and invigorated the plot and left Fletcher's pastoral fancy and exquisite verse unimpaired. How delightful the verse is may be shown by any number of passages. In Clorin's first speech the following lines are typical, not exceptional :

> " My meat shall be what these wild woods afford,
> Berries and chestnuts, plantains, on whose cheeks
> The sun sits smiling, and the lofty fruit
> Pulled from the fair head of the straight-grown pine."

Delightful as is such verse to read, it might be thought likely to prove ineffective in the theatre. On the contrary, the audience found itself hanging upon the words, charmed and fascinated by the music of the verse as it fell from the lips of the players. The dramatic tension tightened or loosened with the colour of the verse. Miss Isabel Jeans was able to make Cloe amuse or thrill us at will. When she said :

> " Here be woods as green
> As any ; air likewise as fresh and sweet
> As where smooth Zephyrus plays on the fleet
> Face of the curled streams."

we were lulled as by music. When she passed
into another key :

> " Choose where thou wilt, whilst I sit by and sing,
> Or gather rushes, to make many a ring
> For thy long fingers; tell the tales of love—
> How the pale Phœbe, hunting in a grove,
> First saw the boy Endymion, from whose eyes
> She took eternal fire that never dies;
> How she conveyed him softly in a sleep,
> His temples bound with poppy, to the steep
> Head of old Latmus, where she stoops each night
> Gilding the mountain with her brother's light
> To kiss her sweetest . . ."

we were caught in a moment as dramatic, by
virtue of its relative passionate cadence in the
smooth pastoral verse, as any Pineroesque or
Guitry climax in a modern play. Then there
are moments of pure dramatic beauty such as we
never get in any modern play. That moment
when Clorin, startled, cries out :

> " Shepherd, how cam'st thou hither to this place ?
> No way is trodden; all the verdant grass
> The spring shot up stands yet unbruised here
> Of any foot; only the dappled deer
> Far from the feared sound of crooked horn
> Dwells in this fastness."

With this loveliness—and how much lovelier it
is spoken *in situ* you cannot imagine !—goes a
nimble wit which delights us in Cloe's lines :

> " For from one cause of fear I am most free,
> It is impossible to ravish me,
> I am so willing."

63

Can there be greater nonsense than is affirmed by some critics, who will have it that there is no place in the theatre for words ? This arbitrary narrowing of " action " to some sort of physical diarrhœa —seen in its most acute form in a type of melodrama where detectives and crooks chase each other to the accompaniment of door-slammings, wall- and table-rappings, wind-blown curtains, expiring lamps and diabolical shrieks—is one of the strangest illusions of the age, and it persists only because the public gets no chance of seeing and expressing its approval of plays which depart from the Anglo-French convention of the last fifty years. I cannot believe that the public would not enjoy *The Faithful Shepherdess* as produced by the Phœnix Society if it were given the chance. It would be advisable to cut it, as at present it plays for at least half-an-hour too long ; but this done, then, with its present cast and setting and with Sir Thomas Beecham in charge of the music, I think it would be commercially successful even if we must remember that on its first appearance it was a failure and that Ben Jonson wrote :

> " . . . thy murdered poem : which shall rise
> A glorified work to time, when fire
> Or moths shall eat what all these fools admire."

There are plenty of fools still who may not admire *The Faithful Shepherdess*, but let us hope there are to-day enough who can admire to fill a theatre for a few months.

THE MASTERSINGERS

WAGNER made the first sketch of the poem of *The Mastersingers*, in the little house " Asyl " bought for him on the Wesendoncks' estate, near Lake Zürich, on Good Friday, 1857. He was then forty-four, and he writes in his Autobiography :

"Now its noble possibilities struck me with overwhelming force, and out of my thoughts about Good Friday, I rapidly conceived a whole drama, of which I made a rough sketch with a few dashes of the pen, dividing the whole into three acts."

He then proceeded to the composition of the second act of *Siegfried,* and much of the forest scene of that opera was conceived during the daily walks he was accustomed to take in the peaceful woods of the Sihltahl. The composition of *Siegfried* was then interrupted by the composition of the poem of *Tristan.* It is amusing to read Wagner's disingenuous comment made about this time on his increasing intimacy with the

Wesendoncks: "Curiously enough, this closer association with my neighbour coincided with the time when I began to work out my libretto, *Tristan and Isolda*."

Much was to happen before the idea of *The Mastersingers* was to recur to Wagner. At the beginning of the year 1858 he found himself too restless to begin the instrumentation of the first act of *Tristan*, and determined to leave "Asyl" on one of his characteristic tours. He went to Paris, where he heard for the first time in his life, Haydn's *Seasons*; of the performance he merely remarks maliciously that the audience thought the florid vocal cadences "very original and charming." In Paris he heard that Berlioz was busy composing a grand opera, *The Trojans*. Berlioz was probably the only one of Wagner's contemporaries in whose music Wagner ever showed the slightest genuine interest, and it is depressing to read the peculiar way in which Wagner refers to this opera:

> "In order to get an impression of the work I was particularly anxious to hear the libretto Berlioz had written himself, and he spent an evening reading it out to me. I was disappointed in it, not only as far as it was concerned, but also by its singularly dry and theatrical delivery. I fancied that in the latter I could see the character of the music to which he had set the words, and I sank

66

into utter despair about it, as I could see that he regarded this as his masterpiece, and was looking forward to its production as the great object of his life."

Of course we must not accept Wagner's valuation of *The Trojans*. It is always necessary in reading Wagner to say softly to oneself, every other sentence, " You liar ! " The complexity of Wagner's character was such that he himself could scarcely have unravelled the mixture of motives behind almost every word he uttered. One day, when musical criticism has developed into a real exercise of thought, someone will study the respective careers of Berlioz and Wagner, and explain to us how it was that Wagner —who had only a six years' longer life than Berlioz —developed so much more satisfactorily and completely.

In the spring of 1858 Wagner returned to Zürich and began again on *Tristan*, which he continued working at during that summer, until his rupture with the Wesendoncks in August. The composition of *Tristan* was continued that autumn at Venice, until the second act was completed, about the middle of March, 1859. But it is characteristic of Wagner that he could not stay six months in Venice without taking a lengthy excursion somewhere, and during that winter he made a train journey to Viterbo, near Rome, in order to get some exercise by walking inland for several miles. On leaving Venice in March, after a trip to Milan and a visit to Zürich, he settled down in Lucerne at the Hotel Schweizerhof, and during that summer completed *Tristan* there. Then he felt he must move again, so he wrote to his wife, whom he had not seen for a year, inviting her to meet him in Paris, where he proposed to make a home. He also needed money to live, but he managed to obtain this from Wesendonck. He arrived in Paris in September, 1859, and took a villa on a three years' agreement, in the Rue Newton, at a rental of four thousand francs a year. Wagner states that he then looked upon himself as a resident of Paris for the rest of his life. In Paris Wagner gave several concerts, met Rossini, Baudelaire, Champfleury and " a Russian Count Tolstoi," who, he says, " was conspicuously kind." In March, 1860, he went to Brussels, where he gave two concerts. On his return to Paris most of his energies were given up to preparing for the famous production of *Tannhäuser*, at the Paris Opera House. In August he set out on a fresh excursion into Germany, and, among other towns, touched at Frankfort. On this stay in Frankfort Wagner writes :

> " When I was there it occurred to me that this was the residence of Schopenhauer, but a singular timidity restrained me from calling upon him. My temper just then seemed

too distraught, and too far removed from all that might have formed a subject for conversation with Schopenhauer, even if I had felt strongly attracted towards him, which alone could have furnished a reason for intruding myself upon him, in spite of such disinclination. As with so many other things in my life, I again deferred one of its most precious opportunities, until that fervently expected 'more favourable season,' which I presumed was sure to come some day. When, a year after this flying visit, I again stayed some time in Frankfort to superintend the production of my *Meistersinger*, I imagined that at last this more favourable opportunity for seeing Schopenhauer had come. But, alas ! he died that very year, a fact which led me to many bitter reflections on the uncertainty of fate."

Here, it will be observed, is some confusion of dates, for in 1861 *The Mastersingers* was not even begun. On his return to Paris that autumn he met the young banker, Emil Erlanger, who helped him financially, and at the end of the year he composed the Paris version of the Venusberg music of *Tannhäuser*. In the spring of 1861 came the famous production of the opera at the Paris House, when the members of the Jockey Club created such an uproar. In April Wagner left Paris and set out on his travels once again.

At the end of the year he met the Wesendoncks in Venice :

> " They seemed to have no desire to realise my position in Vienna (non-production of *Tristan*). Indeed, after the ill-success of my Paris undertaking, entered upon with such glorious anticipations, I had learned to recognise amongst most of my friends a tacitly submissive abandonment of all hope for my future success."

But note the conclusion of this, for nothing shows the remarkable quality of the " unsuccessful " Wagner, aged forty-eight, more than the following :

> " Wesendonck, who always went about armed with huge field-glasses, and was ever ready for sight-seeing, only once took me with him to see the Academy of Arts, a building which, on my former visit to Venice, I had only known from the outside. In spite of all my indifference, I must confess that the ' Assumption of the Virgin,' by Titian, exercised a most sublime influence over me, so that as soon as I realised its conception, my old power revived within me, as though by a sudden flash of inspiration.
>
> " I determined at once on the composition of the *Meistersinger*."

Wagner at once left for Vienna, where, he says, his most urgent need was " to secure some means of livelihood during the composition of my work." He applied first to the music publisher, Schott, of Mayence, offering him literary and performing rights of the new work to be composed for twenty thousand francs, but " a telegram from Schott, containing an absolute refusal, at once destroyed all hope." It is amusing to think that this sort of thing still goes on, that if there is to-day anywhere in Europe a really original genius you may be sure that he is confronting the same difficulties as Wagner faced. I think that a tablet should be erected on the front of the theatre at Bayreuth, containing, engraved in letters of gold, the names of all those men and women who, during the first fifty years of Wagner's life, lent him or gave him money, for it is to them that we owe *The Mastersingers*, the *Ring*, and *Tristan and Isolda*.

In December, 1861, Wagner arrived once more at Paris, and took " a modest room " at the Hotel Voltaire, on the quay of the same name. There, hiding himself from most of his acquaintances, he began and finished the libretto of *The Mastersingers*. When this was concluded he left Paris on February 1st, 1862, for Karlsruhe, and hoped to begin composing the music in quiet solitude at Biebrich, near Mayence. But he could not recover his working mood and left for Baden. Later on towards the summer he writes :

71

"The fair season of the year was now approaching, and I was once more seized with a desire for work. As from the balcony of my flat in a sunset of great splendour I gazed upon the magnificent spectacle of 'Golden' Mayence, with the majestic Rhine pouring along its outskirts in a glory of light, the prelude to my *Meistersinger* again suddenly made its presence closely and distinctly felt in my soul. Once before had I seen it rise before me out of a lake of sorrow, like some distant mirage. I proceeded to write down the prelude exactly as it appears to-day in the score, that is, containing the clear outlines of the leading themes of the whole drama."

By the autumn Wagner had not yet finished the first act. In October he went to Leipzig and Dresden. In order to raise money he gave concerts in Vienna and St. Petersburg in 1862. In 1863 he had got no further, and when King Ludwig of Bavaria stepped in and saved him in 1864, *The Mastersingers* had not been touched again. Wagner was then fifty-one years old.

When listening to *The Mastersingers* we do well to have some conception of the length of time which elapsed between the first undertaking of that work and its final execution. It is difficult to know which is the more amazing, the marvellous *inspired* character of the work in its conception, or the stupendous vitality of its creator, who, in the face of all obstacles, persisted slowly in his intentions, and was finally rewarded by reaching his goal.

POPULAR MUSIC AND DRAMA

THE problem of how society can best
support the arts is surely becoming more
and more acute. It ought to be, it is
assumed to be, comparatively simple. Good art
ought to be able to pay its way. It ought not
to need subsidising, it ought not, perhaps, even
to need advertisement, but in practice almost
everybody concedes the advantage of advertisement. But advertisement itself is only a form of
subsidy. You cannot make known anything to
anybody by a simple announcement. You have
got to put your placard where it will be seen,
you have got to ensure its being read; when
read it must be understood. It contains a message, but how is the message to be comprehended?
The simplest sentence is liable, if not to miscon-
struction, to non-construction—it may produce
no effect. How can one *not* fail? Well, one can
employ a Master of Advertisement, one who can
rivet the attention of the passer-by and make
him understand that you have something so
precious to give him that he runs to meet you in
your picture-gallery or your theatre or your
opera-house. But Masters of Advertisement are

expensive, and they are mostly not masters, but quacks and frauds, and fill your theatre with people who having come once do not come again ; for they have been deceived, they did not read your advertisement aright, or rather they read it aright, for your quack-master did not announce *you* but some other.

Probably it is best to go on without any advertisement, but this is the most expensive of all ways of advertising. It means putting something good before the public week after week, month after month, year after year, while the public slowly learns that it is there. It is one prolonged advertisement at the cost of human lives. If those men and women can find sustenance in the meantime, then they may be able to go on until the value of their offerings is known and paid for. How are they to do this ? It can only be done when it can be done individually. One individual man or woman may be able so to manipulate his life as to achieve a certain proportion of the work he desired to do. But when an organisation of many men and women has to be sustained it is quite a different matter. Then we can expect nothing but mediocre work unless the organisation is adequately subsidised.

The other day Mr. William Archer and Mr. H. Granville-Barker wrote a letter to *The Times* on the subject of the amount of money required for the National Theatre, which—unless there is a European catastrophe—nothing can prevent our having within the next ten, possibly five, years. Mr. Archer is determined to have it, Mr. Granville-Barker is determined to have it, I am determined to have it, the Shakespeare National Memorial Committee is determined to have it, the British Drama League is determined to have it, and in time our united fury of desire will force it upon the British public as the Education Act of 1870 was forced upon the British public.

The first result of the millions being taught to read and write has been the swamping of good literature by bad. Obviously the advent of a new public of millions whose grandfathers could not write their own names has created the popular Press and the popular book, but it has also added a handful of readers every year to the intelligentsia, and that handful will grow. Nothing can stop the progress of our intellects. The children of those who read *John Bull* will read the *Nation* or the *New Statesman*. Mr. J. Middleton Murry, moved to sympathy with their struggles, has already provided them with a stepping-stone in the *Adelphi ;* in two generations they will take in and try to understand Mr. T. S. Eliot's poems in the *Criterion*, and the children of those few enterprising souls will be sent to Cambridge and become Fellows of King's, inheriting the traditions of Mr. J. Maynard Keynes and Mr. Edward J. Dent. That is as far as we need go, and it will be as far as they will go. Their offspring will cause nobody any trouble. But we shall not have to wait so long to receive the benefits of the National Theatre when opened, nor will they be so esoteric when they come. The theatre will have a governing body and, I personally hope, Mr. Granville-Barker as director and despot. It will be as impervious to the clamour of the popular Press as the Poet Laureate was to the demands of the *Daily Mail* that he should write more epithalamia or odes for coronations and other festivals. It is nevertheless possible, however improbable, that although intelligent, you may fail to see the advantage of a National Theatre. You may ask unimaginatively, as a writer in the popular Press may be relied upon to ask any day, Why should we want a National Theatre?

If we spend millions per annum on elementary education without expecting a monetary return on our outlay, it is at least reasonable that we should spend a few thousands per annum on higher education. Of all the forms of higher education the theatre is the most socially advantageous. It is difficult—although no one doubts it would be beneficial—to get the young man or young woman, after leaving school between the eager impressionable ages of fifteen and twenty-five, to enter a public library or an art gallery. Yet in spite of the fact that not one in one thousand of the youth of London ever enters the National Gallery, the British Museum, the South Kensington Museums or the Tate or Wallace

Collections, no one proposes that these institutions should be shut up and the money saved spent on poison gas. It is recognised that the bread is cast upon the waters, and all we demand is that it should be bread and not a stone. For example, a proposal to sell all the old masters in the National Gallery and replace them by copies, although it would raise millions, would not even be popular. That small fraction of the adolescent public to whom these galleries and museums are sustenance and delight are the apostles of civilisation and the hope of the future. But it is far easier to get the young man into a theatre than into a museum or library. It is also more generally beneficial if the theatre is of the same standing dramatically as, let us say, our National Gallery is pictorially. This being really irrefutable it would seem strange to a Martian that we should possess public libraries, a British Museum, a National Gallery, but no National Theatre, when a National Theatre is obviously an even more important public service. We would not allow our National Gallery to be run by fortune-hunting picture-dealers, or our public libraries by the proprietors of the *Daily Mail ;* why then do we allow the theatre to be completely at the mercy of every Tom, Dick and Harry to speculate with entirely for his private gain and regardless of any obligation to his fellow-men ?

Our neglect of the theatre as a public service is due to the puritanical traditions which associated the theatre with the World, the Flesh, and the Devil. I agree with Mr. Bernard Shaw when he said : " Only the ablest critics believe that the theatre is really important : in my time none of them would claim for it, as I claim for it, that it is as important as the Church was in the Middle Ages and much more important than the Church in London." And Miss Jane Harrison, in that admirable book, *Ancient Art and Ritual*, expresses a similar idea when she says : " It is at the outset the same impulse that sends a man to church and to the theatre."

But I do not wish just now to touch upon the religious nature of art. The Age of Bloomsbury with its highly Significant Forms among the London intelligentsia is still upon us. They do not believe in anything later than the eighteenth century, and in the eighteenth century the theatre was a plaything, although a delightful plaything. Well, they shall have their plaything, and the twentieth century will secretly try to contribute something of its own. If the new generation is going to sweep the trivialities, the intellectual buffoonery of Bloomsbury into the dust-heap, where lie the parsonical solemnities of Mr. Samuel Smiles—who would have considered any young man who entered a theatre as beyond self-help— let us at least give them a stage whereon the farce, melodrama or divine comedy may be enacted.

79

Briefly, what I and thousands of inarticulate young men want to see is a National Theatre in London which shall consist, in the same block of buildings, of two houses—one small and one fairly large, equipped with a studio for scenery and properties. In the larger house we should, I hope, see performances of *The Ring*, of Shakespeare's plays and of other English and Foreign drama; the smaller house to be used for Purcell, Gluck, Mozart, Gilbert and Sullivan, ancient and modern comedy, and marionette comedy, opera and ballet. Such a show as the Sir Thomas Beecham and the Phœnix Society's production of Fletcher's *The Faithful Shepherdess*, instead of being performed privately to a small society, would find its natural home in the National Theatre. The plays of Tchekov, for example, which the public will never see without a National Theatre, would be constantly in the repertory. Such a masterpiece as Mr. Shaw's *Heartbreak House* would not remain completely inaccessible as at present. But there is no end to the list that might be drawn up. What is equally important is that when we get this National Theatre we shall not only hear and see the best of the music and drama of the past, but that an opportunity will be given to all our actors, musicians and artists to show what they can do. The National Theatre would not give us a stereotyped *Cymbeline* (even that would be better than none at all as at present), it would give us a

Granville-Barker plus Norman Wilkinson *Cymbeline*, then a Nigel Playfair plus Albert Rutherston *Cymbeline*, then somebody else's *Cymbeline*. The same would apply to the acting. All good actors would have their chance to show what they could do. Naturally there would be terrific rows. There would be columns of abuse of this and the other. But nothing could be healthier. There is nothing pleases a robust artist so much as denunciation and abuse. When we have the *Daily Mail* and the *Daily Express* at each other's throats over a production by Mr. Granville-Barker at the National Theatre we shall be able to sing *Nunc Dimittis*. As for Mr. Granville-Barker, or whoever is in charge of the National Theatre, he will not turn a hair. He will give us one day a comedy by Mr. George Moore and another a tragedy by Tolstoy, and we shall be either furious or blissfully happy. Sir Thomas Beecham, or whoever is in charge of the musical side, will be equally provocative. Then we shall have a really live theatre. London will be so exciting a place to live in that the provincial towns will at once start Municipal theatres, and try to coax our National Theatre companies to visit them lest their own population completely abandon them for the capital. All this can come to pass in a few years. All that is wanted is one million pounds—the price of a room in the National Gallery.

"We don't want that sort of highbrow stuff!"

declared a member of the Shakespeare Memorial National Theatre Committee whose support I had hoped to win. His opinion is that of the majority of Fleet Street journalists who are, I always think, less in touch with the public mind than any other group in the community, since they always mistake ancient prejudice for contemporary thought, and their motto is " *Do not lead, follow !* "

His opinion is one that may imply an attitude to the theatre that is hopeless and paralysing, or it may be due to a misunderstanding of the ideas of people like myself who want a National Theatre. The word " highbrow " is one of those usefully vague words which can be stuck on to anything or anybody one dislikes. If you suspect a man of knowing more than you yourself do on any subject, fling the epithet " highbrow " at him and his superiority is at once undermined. It is good to have such a weapon, for we have all in our time suffered from the cold-blooded indifference of prigs and superior persons to our need to gratify our own low tastes. But neither I nor any other ardent supporter of the National Theatre is trying to deprive the ordinary man of his ordinary theatre. I am not even advocating the compulsory closure of all the cinemas in the United Kingdom, although I would as soon spend a night in Hell as an evening in a cinema. My tastes are low, obviously ! The world frequents the cinema, and, therefore, in a democracy, the man who loathes what all the world admires is a low fellow—to call him a highbrow is the most biting sarcasm.

Nor do I want to hold meetings outside cinemas exhorting people not to run with such alacrity to the devil, although I sincerely believe that in frequenting the cinema they are dulling their senses, stupefying their brains and clouding their imaginations—all of which means that they *are* going to the devil very rapidly !

All I want is to see their type die out quickly and be replaced by something better, by men and women who do not guffaw like a herd of ourang-outangs at feeble jokes. But I don't think any the worse of the ourang-outang or of his human brother. We shall all be ourang-outangs to somebody, I hope. What we need not be is ourang-outangs to ourselves, and that is what I should be if I pretended that the ordinary London theatre was good enough for me. Well, if it isn't good enough for me, surely it is presumptuous impertinence and the grossest priggishness for me to declare that it is good enough for everybody else. That would be " superiority " if you like ! But, then, my critic interrupts with " Tchekov ! You want the plays of Tchekov performed at the National Theatre ! " I can but reply that at the end of Mr. Komisarjevsky's production of *Uncle Vanya* at the Stage Society I could only grope blindly for my hat. I was so moved that if anybody had spoken to me I should have burst into tears. And who am I to think that Tchekov wrote only for me?

My critic adds that Englishmen will never understand the plays of Tchekov because Englishmen and Russians are so utterly different in character. The gentleman who said this to me added in the same breath that Tchekov was one of the greatest short-story writers in the world. But if Englishmen can understand Tchekov's short stories, they can understand his plays. Tchekov did not write about Englishmen in his short stories and about Russians in his plays.

I am not going to say how many Englishmen can understand Tchekov. I don't care if they only number half-a-dozen. Nothing could alter the fact that the National Theatre would be for this half-dozen and not for the ourang-outangs who prefer *Kiki*, a typically dull "lively" play which had great success in England and America. To build and establish a National Theatre for them would be a comic extravagance. They have got the theatre they want. What fatuous folly, then, to spend a million upon providing them with what they already possess. Nor do we want a National Theatre to improve the masses. I have no belief in this improvement business. The intelligent, the sensitive, those who can appreciate the best the dramatists, actors and other artists of the theatre can provide, will be found in the National Theatre; those who can't will be at *Kiki*. I believe the intelligent and sensitive are more numerous than Fleet Street imagines, but I am not going to support a National Theatre that is to play down to the masses in the hope of slowly educating them. That is sheer lunacy. Do that and the masses themselves will despise you, for they have an instinct that is sounder than the intelligence of Fleet Street, an instinct which guides them even when they do not understand.

The policy of Fleet Street and of the superficial intelligence which it represents is the policy of those who do not care. They have no passion for the theatre. They assert glibly that the Slav melancholy of Tchekov is utterly foreign to Englishmen, as if the English were an inferior race incapable of melancholy, as if unhappiness were not stamped upon the faces you meet walking along the Strand. These critics do not realise that we who want the National Theatre do not want within its walls people who cannot be unhappy.

The whole virtue of a National Theatre is that it would be subsidised and independent of the *canaille* who may be inhabiting London hotels or London hovels. God forbid that we should ever have a National Theatre that would satisfy the editor of a popular newspaper, whose ideal is to please more readers than anyone else. There is a sense in which we may take to ourselves the epithet " highbrow " as the highest of compliments.

A " highbrow " in this sense is a man who believes in his own thoughts and feelings and does not attempt to trim his policy according to what he guesses may be the thoughts and feelings of the majority. Whether in politics or art, mankind knows the latter type to its cost. It is the " trimmer," the charlatan ; the often well-meaning humbug ; the man who, in trying to please everybody, in the end pleases nobody, and makes a complete hash of things. We are not going to have a National Theatre run on those lines. We are going to have a National Theatre run by a man in whom we can have complete confidence. That is why I say I hope to see Mr. Granville-Barker as its head. I differ profoundly from Mr. Granville-Barker in many things. Mr. Granville-Barker will probably detest many of the plays I like, but Mr. Granville-Barker is not a " trimmer," or a demagogue, or a man with his ear to the ground in that most fantastically foolish of all endeavours—the attempt to discover the feeble pulsations of the great heart of the public ! The National Theatre does not need as its head a " perfect " director ; all it needs is a real artist and not a trifler, an artist who, in utter sincerity, will go his own way, whether it be popular or unpopular. In such a man directing such a theatre, the whole public, whether high- or low-brow, will have instinctive confidence. As the public learns to know him and his theatre—and the whole point of having a National Theatre is that it will have a succession of such directors—it will come to see what he does. It may or may not understand, but it will feel excited about his work, for the quality of the sincere artist is that he excites interest. Then I expect to live to see an audience at the National Theatre enraptured at the beauty of a performance of *The Tempest* or *A Midsummer Night's Dream*, and rising from a performance of *Uncle Vanya* shaken to the depths of their souls by the poignancy of that profound and terrible play.

At the " Promenades," with perhaps the solitary exception of Wagner, Bach and Beethoven may be truthfully said to be the most popular of all composers. An enthusiastic democrat might hail this fact as proof of the popularity of good art. But the Promenade public itself is a small group of Londoners interested in music, a mere fraction of the masses who habitually listen to music of some kind or other every week in London. Would those masses be able to appreciate Bach and Beethoven ? It may seem an idle question, since they do not bother to go to hear Bach and Beethoven, although the " Promenades " have now been an annual event in London for more than a quarter of a century. But if they do not bother to go to hear Bach and Beethoven, still less do they bother to go to hear Dvořák, Berlioz, Gounod, Rossini, Gluck or Verdi on the Tuesdays, Wednesdays or Thursdays at the " Promenades." On the contrary, those audiences are largely made up of the same people who go on Fridays to hear Bach and Beethoven, people whose interest in music is strong enough to extend to composers of the second or third class. I believe that the intellectually alert minority is not only the sole support of all that is best in art, but also of all that is second and third best. The great bulk of the people is apathetic and goes wherever it is easiest to go. The masses simply take the line of least resistance. This is proved over and over again. If it were only true of music, it would mean nothing, for one cannot expect everybody to be musical; but it is true of every art and of every phase of life. Yet year after year goes by, and in spite of all experience we have the same sorry spectacle of reformers or pioneers kowtowing to the multitude, abjectly apologising for their own unpopularity, humbly promising to be less highbrow, declaring that they only wish to please the masses and to promote the well-being of the masses, and the masses continue to treat their effusive flattery and their spineless toadying and cajolery with the contempt it deserves.

I am accused of being arrogantly highbrow and contemptuous of the ordinary man. Well, I think the most contemptuous, the most insulting way of behaving to the ordinary man is to attempt to write down to him. When I hear actors or musicians or writers saying the public knows what is good, the public is " all right "—generally preparatory to the exposition of some scheme whose avowed object is to improve the public—I am seized with nausea at such hypocritical effrontery. The public does not know what is good, it does not even care to know; it is *not* " all right," it is lazy, stupid, indifferent, apathetic and incapable of sustained desire, effort or discipline. Everything of value that has ever been produced in this world has been the creation of a passionate, persistent minority. All our laws, our very conceptions of honour, of justice, of morality, of virtue, we owe to a handful of superior minds. All our art, our literature, our music, our knowledge, we owe again to a small band of explorers adventuring where their fellows could not even dream of venturing—bringing back treasure for each one of us. Of all the many sickening forms of cant, this " democratic " flattery of the ignorant, bullying, sheep-like multitude is the grossest and most loathsome. Every honest man will admit that at the end of all his endeavours (however successful !) just to die and so make room for someone better will be the crowning, perhaps the one real achievement of his life. If the best of men feel thus—and it is undeniable that they do—how can we stoop to that insincere flattery which pretends that what the miserable, diseased, undeveloped specimens of *Homo sapiens* living in the slums, suburbs and ant-heaps of 1924, oppressed and depressed, desire is what is most desirable ?

Yet I would affirm that what all men without

exception in their hearts desire is exactly what the greatest men of all time have desired, if the majority only understood themselves better ; but they are ignorant, they do not know. In the words of Milton : " The hungry sheep look up and are not fed." Restlessly they pour night after night into a thousand cinemas and devour with their eyes a thousand daily and weekly " rags " which flatter their weaknesses, lull them into a false contentment with their habits, their tastes and their opinions when they should be telling them the truth, which is that as they are *they are unfit to live.*

If I were a director of a National Theatre I should boldly proclaim my contempt for the present taste of the public. I should have in bold plain letters upon every bill, poster and advertisement :

TO THE MULTITUDE.
THIS IS TOO GOOD FOR YOU.
DON'T COME !

That is the only possible policy for a real artist, and what a magnificent policy to have to live up to ! Everything you did would have to be really too good. It would strain every nerve, every capacity of yourself and your fellow-artists to stay at that level. And how the public would pour in their masses upon you ! There are few men whose spirit is so dead that they would not respond to such a challenge. But you would have to make them believe that your contempt for them was real. It would have to be real to be successful. As a mere stunt such a policy would be an abject failure. Also, though many would come, few would remain. But those few would, in this city of seven millions, be sufficient to fill nightly our National Theatre. The influence of its excellence would spread as the influence of the Christian ideal spread, in spite of the constant backsliding of the average man. Then when the National Theatre was firmly established, when it had become a popular institution, when nearly everyone had become a national theatre-goer, just as nearly everyone in modern Europe became a Christian, you would have to start a new movement, a reformation of the National Theatre, which movement would have its origin in contempt for the lifeless mediocrity and dullness of the popular National Theatre. But the good work done would remain. It would have provided a foundation, and without a foundation of some sort nothing can be built at all.

MARIONETTE OPERA

DURING a season in London at the Scala Theatre, Cav. Fidora and Dr. Podrecca's puppets from the Teatro dei Piccoli, Rome, gave a number of operas. They made a beginning with Respighi's *The Sleeping Beauty*. Respighi is one of the leading Italian composers of the day. His orchestrated version of Rossini's music in the Russian ballet, *La Boutique Fantasque*, is well known and some of his orchestral works have been performed in London. Musically, *The Sleeping Beauty* is not of exceptional merit; it is well made but lacking in character. But there is some excellently invented puppet-play in this opera; for example, a procession of mourners, a ballet of green Lilliputians, and a scene of spiders spinning their webs across the Enchanted Castle. None of these episodes could be obtained quite so effectively, if at all, in flesh and blood opera, but otherwise a certain strange comicality, characteristic of puppet-shows, is chiefly what distinguishes this marionette opera from the ordinary human affair.

It would seem that there is nothing which the actor or singer on the stage can do that cannot be done by puppets, except speaking or singing; but at the same time some things undergo a subtle transformation. Imagine Mozart's *Figaro* played by puppets, and nothing would seem to be lost. In fact, I think *Figaro* ought always to be performed as a puppet opera, because the singers, being hidden behind the scenes, could always be selected solely for their voices. What matters most in *Figaro* is the singing and the playing—the rest is pure comedy, and in pure comedy the human being has already been eliminated. The characters of *Figaro* are already types, abstractions, *puppets*. What about Puccini? Let us imagine *La Bohème* as a puppet opera! Here once more I think we should gain rather than lose. Do you think a little of the sentiment attached to Mimi would go? I assure you nothing is so touching as a wistful puppet maiden in rags who has fallen in love with a puppet artist in a velvet jacket—especially as Mimi would not need to weigh twenty stone and measure sixty-eight inches round the waist! A puppet in a fall of snow (third act of *La Bohème*) is also extremely pathetic.

No, there is no need for our prima donna of the future to live like Byron on six bottles of soda-water and three biscuits *per diem*; she can have half-a-dozen bottles of Guinness at her side during the whole performance and take raw eggs at frequent intervals, as I remember seeing a famous tenor do when I was a child. Puccini has nothing to fear from the puppets, and I confess I long to see *The Girl of the Golden West* done by Cav. Fidora and Dr. Podrecca's marionettes. I would have it played as a passionate love-drama in the Grand Italian opera manner, but I should let there be no attempt at stylisation. I would have everything realistic—super-Caruso tenors and a super-abundant soprano, all acting as redundantly as possible.

But what about a finer, more genuinely imaginative work? What about Debussy's *Pelléas and Mélisande?* Now, this is where I see the Teatro dei Piccoli marionettes at the Scala Theatre falling short. Their merit is wholly mechanical and is due to their clever manipulation by the operators, whose names are given on the programme as Gorno Bros., Dell' Acqua, Prandi and Corsi. The marionettes themselves are not beautiful or striking. Their costumes are commonplace, the scenery or stage-settings undistinguished. I cannot see them performing *Pelléas and Mélisande* without ruining it. On the other hand, I believe that the perfect performance of *Pelléas and Mélisande* would be given by marionettes. I can imagine puppet figures of such beauty, carved faces of such tranquil loveliness, moving with so dream-like and unhuman a movement through scenery small and exquisite and unreal, that we should sit enchanted, listening to that delicate shimmering music. Here we get a hint of the future possibilities of marionettes.

What could not be done with them if we had the time, money, patience and genius to use them! But who is there to attend to such things in the theatrical scramble for existence of to-day?

Let us return to the contemplation of what does exist; for example, the Wagner operas or music-dramas. Can we imagine them performed by marionettes? *Rienzi*, yes; *The Flying Dutchman*, I think so; *Tannhäuser*, surely, perfectly charming! Imagine the Pilgrims' Chorus, the Venusburg, the puppet minstrels twanging their harps in the Hall of Song! Nobody can be expected to take *Tannhäuser* seriously to-day, and the puppets would subtly change our boredom to laughter without in the least diminishing the effect of the music. *Lohengrin?*—no doubt whatever! But *Rhinegold*, the *Ring?* Yes, I believe a transformation of scale would leave the impressiveness of the *Ring* intact, even augmented. Giant, human and dwarf puppets among all the Wagnerian mechanical contrivances could give us, what human actors can never give us, a perfect performance of the *Ring*. Can you not conceive " The Ride of the Valkyries " with winged puppets actually flying through the air? Make the whole of the *Ring* mechanical, and you have then eliminated the mechanical, and it is the only possible way of eliminating it. At present, the mixture of stage machinery and human beings is a serious artistic flaw and fatally clogs the imagination.

95

But now what about *Tristan and Isolda?* I confess I cannot see this successfully played by marionettes. It is too human, in a sense too intimate and real. It is not love as it is exhibited in Puccini opera, or the dream love of *Pelléas and Mélisande :* it is much more alive and palpitating, and puppets would be strikingly incongruous. Yet I would not be quite convinced about it if I did not remember the long periods of immobility of the two chief personages in *Tristan and Isolda.* For considerable stretches of time they stand or sit almost motionless. Now the lifeless marionette can imitate or suggest human beings *in motion* admirably, but fails most glaringly to represent or suggest them when *in repose.* Immediately a marionette stops moving it becomes idiotically lifeless. There is a very simple explanation of this, namely, that it is precisely by movement that the marionette suggests life; when it cannot move its power is gone. Therefore I think *Tristan and Isolda* is an opera quite outside the scope of marionettes. But it is remarkable that I cannot call to mind another opera that would be inaccessible to marionettes, while most operas, I am convinced, would be far better produced in this way than by the customary company of men and woman.

There is another question to be raised. Is twentieth-century music more suggestive of marionettes than earlier music? The two best known modern composers are Scriabin and Stravinsky. The first is no less emotional than Tchaikovsky; he suggests revival meetings and mob-oratory on a grand histrionic scale. For some obscure reason, this does not suggest the mechanical, although it would seem to be more involuntary and mechanical in its activity than the wire-juggling of puppets. When you pull a puppet-string you at least know what you are doing, but such composers as Scriabin in their ecstatic moments overflow their immediate consciousness. What they do then they cannot always repeat. So they seem to be less intelligent than the puppet operator. Intelligence, then, is the hall-mark of marionette music, so that we can see why it is that we feel at once that the music of to-day has a greater affinity with marionettes than that of yesterday. By intelligence I mean conscious artifice. The music of to-day is more consciously contrived than ever before. That in itself is not bad, but you can be more consciously master of your activity merely by restricting your activity. Compared with Beethoven, Stravinsky is not a rich master; he is master of a different area of consciousness, but I do not think it would be true to say that he was more fully self-conscious than Beethoven. He does seem to me, however, more of an intellectual than Scriabin, and in this respect he is more typical of his age. We therefore find him writing pure marionette opera, such as *The Nightingale*, in which men and women are no longer men and women but strange and fantastic puppets. I prophesy that just as opera is developing and will develop more and more into marionette opera, so we shall find the same thing happen to our drama. This may seem superficially to be a step backwards, but I believe that we shall be more fully men and women after we have seen ourselves for a little while as puppets.

SYNCOPATED–JAZZ–RAGTIME

I HAVE heard many jazz bands at dances and have, without exception, disliked them all. Some of them have been hideously noisy, one of the more particularly detestable of their mannerisms being the saxophone yodelling in which the inferior varieties of jazz bands specialise. This yodelling is accompanied by an up-and-down movement of the player's head and instrument, and a side-to-side swaying of the body; meanwhile a ceaseless din is maintained as a sort of *basso ostinato* by a horde of percussion instruments, whose assaulters also sway from side to side and nod their heads as if drunk with their own noise. A larger band will include a cornet or, more excusably, a trumpet, from which ear-splitting coruscations will emerge from time to time, the instrument being strained to the top of its compass and beyond, nothing less than a toneless shriek being thought sufficiently penetrating. Anyone who has ever danced to such a band will agree when I say that it is extremely exhausting—that is, if you are at all sensitive to sound. The worst of these bands—such as those to which hundreds of enthusiasts dance nightly at the Hammersmith Palais de Danse—generally maintain a dead level of *fortissimo* from eight o'clock till midnight. They are idolaters of the god Rhythm, and have no ear for tone. Even their rhythms are for the most part extremely crude and their syncopation is usually of the most banal. I expect that many of these players imagine that syncopation was invented yesterday. They have never heard the " jazz " movement in Franck's *Symphonic Variations ;* of course, syncopation did not begin with Franck; it is as old as the hills, but Franck and Brahms, to name no others, have used syncopated rhythms in a way that leaves all the modern jazz masters standing.

I am not at all impressed by the rhythmic prowess of even the very best of these new jazz or syncopated bands, although the best of them are as superior to those I have been mentioning as the Queen's Hall Orchestra is superior to an ordinary park string band. Whiteman's, which was playing at the Hippodrome recently, was, no doubt, a star syncopated band. I did not hear it, but I heard the negro band at the London Pavilion in the *Dover Street to Dixie* revue, and this was by far the best jazz band I had ever heard. The music they played was not remarkable, except in the first rather long and complicated song sung by Miss Florence Mills. Here there were a number of excellent effects. I don't mean by " effects " that miscellaneous array of unnamable instruments which are part of the machinery of the more elaborate bands. I mean musical effects got by a combination of harmony and rhythm. Musically that song was far in advance of the majority of the new British and foreign compositions that are performed at the " Promenades." The players apparently had no music before them, and I should not be surprised if what I heard was the result of a long collaboration among them. Some composer or " arranger " must have provided the original skeleton idea, the foundation for what ultimately was produced, but I imagine that it had been varied and added to and embroidered by individual players, and that every night as they played there would be some noticeable differences in detail. The sense of rhythm shown by this band was much more subtle than usual, and the freedom of development and variation of the themes was remarkable.

If my surmise is correct, then we have in this and similar bands a musical activity analogous to the drama of the famous Commedia dell' Arte, when actors made up their plays by a highly-developed technique of " gagging." Perhaps such concerted improvisation can occur in the maturity of an art, but if the best jazz-band music to-day is produced in this way, it is chiefly because the composers who are going to make the most of these new musical combinations have not yet arisen. There is, as yet, no tradition of jazz-band music. The players themselves are so scarce that a good saxophone player can command three times the salary of a good violinist. The saxophone is not taught at the Royal College of Music, or at the Royal Academy of Music. Sir Landon Ronald has not even introduced it into the Guildhall School. The musical director of one of these jazz-band organisations informed me—after asking me what I thought of the saxophone as an instrument—that, in his opinion, the perfect saxophone player was not yet born. The present player is either a good reader with a bad tone, or a bad reader with a good tone, or a good reader with a good tone who has not got the peculiar jazz temperament. There is at present among the higher ranks of jazz musicians in England a revolt against the term "jazz." My musical director calls his latest band a syncopated band, and thus tries to define the difference between the noisy type of band and the more musicianly, more polished, more agreeable variety. But "jazz" is a far better description than "syncopated." Syncopation is merely irregular accent and has been a familiar rhythmic device in music and verse throughout history; but "jazz" is not a rhythmic term, it is a new word which serves admirably to describe a special combination of instruments and the special type of music produced by that combination.

The primary function of the jazz band to-day is to provide music for dancing, so that to sit and listen in an empty ball-room to a jazz band playing through its repertory, as I did the other night, is not the ideal way of judging it. Listening to it as a band, I naturally was specially critical of the musical result from a purely æsthetic standpoint. No doubt the finest jazz band, and the finest jazz music, theoretically speaking, would satisfy the musician and the dancer equally. At their highest development the dancing ideal and the musical ideal will fuse together and become one. But we are a long way from that stage yet, and so I emphasise the point that what I am just going to say about jazz music is said from the musical and not the dancing point of view.

What struck me immediately after hearing four or five items from the band's programme was the monotony due to the repeated exploitation of the same small range of effects.

As I sat listening to what was undoubtedly excellent playing, I found myself easily imagining all sorts of variations and developments which that peculiar assembly of instruments cried aloud for. No musician, with an orchestral imagination and the special temperament that delights in plangent rhythm and colour and queer-toned contrasts, could have sat listening to those players without itching to handle that combination more effectively. It is curious that the imagination should have to wait upon the mechanism in this way. Listening to a symphony orchestra, the musical imagination spontaneously conceives music of quite a different character from that suggested by a jazz-band combination. Still more curiously, the imagination may have a certain bias and for long not be able to find the right instrument. This, I should hazard, was the experience of Stravinsky. Listen to Stravinsky's earliest works, written when a musical student accustomed to the usual modern symphony orchestra! His early works are conceived in the terms of that orchestra, but the medium is not natural to him; he can do little more than imitate his predecessors. Then slowly you find him feeling his way to the instrumental combinations which suit his imagination, which actually stimulate it and set free his creative activity. Stravinsky could write magnificently for the jazz band; of that I feel sure. And when I say "magnificently," I mean he might write for that combination music of great originality and beauty. In fact, Stravinsky has already instinctively found his way to groupings of brass, percussion and wood-wind that resemble a jazz band more nearly than a Beethoven symphony orchestra. Stravinsky is not alone in this. It is a general artistic phase, for we find that the most interesting of living musicians jump to one's mind as potential jazz-band composers. For example, Serge Prokoviev and Manuel de Falla, who represent both extremes of the European continent, are as likely as Stravinsky to produce remarkable works in this form. What astonishes me is that none of our young English composers seem to have been attracted by this new medium. Somewhere, there may be a young man with genius who would like to write some modern equivalent to the great Preludes and Fugues of J. S. Bach, and him I recommend to study the peculiarities of the best type of modern jazz band as we see it in the Savoy-Orpheans, for there are great possibilities here awaiting the right man.

OXFORD'S ANNUAL FESTIVAL OF MUSIC

I ALWAYS come back from a short contact with Oxford musical life filled with envy and respect. Envy of all the undergraduates who, living in that delightful town, have such wonderful opportunities of not only hearing a great wealth and diversity of good music, but also of becoming good musicians themselves by sharing in its production ; and respect for Sir Hugh Allen, the Heather Professor of Music in the University of Oxford, but better known to Londoners as the present head of the Royal College of Music, in succession to Sir Charles Stanford.

I confess that living in the comparative isolation of a listener to, not a maker of music, I have a natural and profound scepticism of the value of all academic professors and heads of scholastic institutions. One is apt to judge them from the mass of their students and to reflect that one will never know those students as they might have been had not the hand of tradition removed their natural imbecilities. Natural imbecility, one imagines, could not be worse than unnatural dullness, but I am afraid it is a mistake to imagine that the natural imbecility of the majority of students at any University or School of Music is ever in the least fresh or original. It is probably, on the contrary, hoary and antique as the generations repeat themselves with that monotony which biologists tell us is the fault of the continuity of the germ-plasm. Even the freaks, the " sports " of each generation are not new; they are, with rare exceptions, repetitions of the freaks of their professor's youth, with such slight deviations from the tradition as to be scarcely noticeable.

But as I sat, in the famous old Sheldonian Theatre—known to Handel, Haydn, and many world-famous musicians since—listening to that entirely amateur chorus and that almost entirely amateur orchestra giving a performance of Parry's *De Profundis* and Vaughan-Williams' *A Sea Symphony* worthy of a great professional organisation, I realised that if such results could be procured from a mass of undergraduates, to most of whom music was only a subsidiary interest, it was a proof that Oxford's musical life was in the right hands. A glance at the list of Choral Services during Festival Week at Christ Church, New College and Magdalen confirms this impression, for among the items are Services by Byrd, Tomkins, Bevin, Purcell, and Gibbons; Anthems by J. S. Bach, Schumann, Palestrina, Orlando Gibbons, Haydn, Mozart and Parry. The Choral Services are, of course, a permanent musical interest at Oxford, but the Festival I heard comprised, in addition to the Parry and Vaughan-Williams works I have mentioned, a performance of Bach's B Minor Mass at the Sheldonian Theatre, a concert by the Choirs of New College, Magdalen and Christ Church at the Town Hall, an orchestral concert by the Oxford Orchestral Society (supplemented by professional wind-players) at the Town Hall, which included Stravinsky's *L'Oiseau de Feu*, Elgar's " Enigma " Variations and Mozart's D Minor pianoforte Concerto (soloist, Miss Myra Hess), and at the Corn Exchange during the same week three Historical Ballets with music from the Fitz-william Virginal Book, from Purcell, and from Bach. These are only the main features of the Festival, which also included chamber concerts and organ recitals.

Of this orgy of music I only heard the performance of the three Historical Ballets in the Corn Exchange, and the Parry and Vaughan-Williams concert at the Sheldonian. Parry's *De Profundis* is a short choral work of austere and attractive design. Mr. Vaughan-Williams' *A Sea Symphony* is a more ambitious work. I had heard it once before and remembered it without depression. As I sat listening to it again I found myself falling under the spell of Sir Hugh Allen (who was conducting it) to such an extent that I began to feel really moved. Sir Hugh Allen infused such life into the singing and the playing and drove the whole thing forward with such exuberance and decision that I was frequently thrilled, for Mr. Vaughan-Williams has set Whitman's words with great accomplishment and has admirably conveyed the grandiose emotional spirit of the text. Presently, however, other instincts got the upper hand. I found myself disliking in recollection the commonplace banality (dare I say trickery?) of the words, and of the music which so faithfully reflected those words :

" Behold the sea itself,
And on its limitless, heaving breast, the ships ;
See where their white sails, bellying in the wind, speckle the green and blue,
See the steamers coming and going, steaming in and out of port,
See the drifters drifting with their oozy and carefully manufactured nets,
See the little and the great leviathan sailing solitary in unfathomable deeps,
See dusky and undulating, the long pennants of smoke,
Behold the sea itself,
And on its limitless, heaving breast, the ships."

Now, into that first stanza I have inserted two lines of my own, invented on the spur of the moment. I venture to think they make no difference whatever to the poem ; and surely there is something amiss with the poem if that is possible. That is not, however, the point I want to make ; my point is that Mr. Vaughan-Williams' music seems to me to be as valuable and as superfluous as my two lines. I cannot see that it expresses anything individual and personal to Mr. Vaughan-Williams. It is comparatively easy to mesmerise oneself with other people's emotions, but an original creative artist has to feel something for himself, and he has to be the first ever to feel it, or he is not a great creative artist. This is not to say that what he writes must be absolutely novel—there is nothing new under the sun in that sense—but it must be unique in the impression it makes and that impression must be new. In judging of any work of art it is largely a question of the degree in which the work conveys this effect of originality that determines its genuineness. I dare say there are a number of slight touches which express Vaughan-Williams and no one else in *A Sea Symphony*—they seem most frequent in the slow movement and conclusion—because Mr. Vaughan-Williams is a musician of genuine sensibility, but they are drowned in an ocean of music that has a generic and not an individual character, and, therefore, *A Sea Symphony* as a whole is negligible as an original work of art, however admirable it may be as an exercise for choral societies and a repository of facile second-hand emotions.

Nothing is more easy or more fatal for an artist to acquire than a pose of simple nobility. I know nothing of Mr. Vaughan-Williams, but his music gives me the impression that he is in danger of losing his real self in what can only be some such pose, for such music as *A Sea Symphony* does not carry conviction. It ought not to be easy for an artist to love humanity, or even one human being. Love that is facile and easy is without value. And about humanitarians in general I have my own private opinion. I think they are all humbugs. Let Mr. Vaughan-Williams give us a little more of his real self in his music; even if it appears at first sight slightly unworthy of the late Mr. Walt Whitman it will, I am sure, prove of more value than this monotonous echo of:

"O soul, thou pleasest me, I thee, . . .

*   *   *

Away, O soul! hoist instantly the anchor!

*   *   *

O my brave soul!"

Let us have done with this self-soul-satisfaction!

THE MODERN SPIRIT

THE first performance of Stravinsky's Rag-time in London with a sort of mimed dance by Lopokova and Massine was tacked on to a cinema show at Covent Garden, advertised by its promoter, Mr. Walter F. Wanger, alternately as the " Super-film " and " The Great Spectacle," *Theodora*. Warned by a considerate management that that ballet was timed to begin about ten o'clock, I took every care to avoid " The Great Spectacle," but owing to the inebriate celerity of a taxi-driver, I arrived at Covent Garden at a quarter to ten just in time to see a leopard slinking mysteriously about the screen, then Theodora in " the potency of her gorgeous beauty "—to use the film-language— about to be strangled. Her strangulation was intercepted by the necessity of giving her last message to the breath-bereaved public filling the interstices of Covent Garden Opera House. The scene faded and on the screen appeared the words : " Wait for me, beloved ! "   I had already had a film glimpse of the beloved stretched out dead, so in this case there was every reason for believing that he would wait ; then we flashed back to Theodora with the strangulatory cord around her neck, only, however, to have that scene blotted out by another message, her final command to the executioner : " Delay not ! I have a tryst to keep."

In the interval—for an interval is granted in which an exhausted audience may recover from these super-films—I was told that I had missed the great scene in which innumerable lions devour the populace : the famished beasts rush into the arena at a moment when it is " black with thousands of rebellious people." It sounds splendid. But what were the feelings of the audience that had come to see this super-film when Massine and Lopokova came on and danced, or, rather, mimed with stiff, clock-work, exaggerated gestures and with a curious sophistication, to the emotionless, bizarre, intellectual grimaces of Stravinsky's music ? Well, some I know giggled uncontrollably until they went off into fits of hysteria. Two women near me I expected every moment to roll convulsed upon the floor. Poor things ! the transition from the warm human, palpitating, all-conquering love—" Delay not ! I have a tryst to keep "—to the inhuman, mechanical, sex-sophistication of the Stravinsky jazz was too much for them. A process which has taken a hundred years to come about, that slow revolution human life has made between Beethoven and Stravinsky, was for them completed in half an hour at Covent Garden Theatre. It was quite enough to make anyone silly. But they would recover in good time, and then they would inevitably range themselves into the two camps: those who look upon "Delay not! I have a tryst to keep" and Beethoven as expressions of the human spirit, infinitely precious and valuable, while regarding Stravinsky as decadent and valueless, and that other party who are bored with Beethoven and think the word "tryst" an abomination, but who leave the Massine-Lopokova rag-time murmuring ecstatically: "How transcendental!"

There will be a few who will object to the conjunction of "Delay not! I have a tryst to keep" with Beethoven, but, though I should be the last to deny that there is a difference, I do maintain that they belong to a world of the same order, and that it is a world that has passed away, even although the majority of men and women in this country may at first sight appear still to belong to it. It is only the low level of intellectual consciousness that prevents the mass of film-seers from recognising the absurd unreality *for them* of the grand passions which are depicted in the three, four, five and six reel dramas which they flock to see.

But although nothing like this gorgeousness of love is to be met with in their daily life, they are not disillusioned. They imagine it is there— the prerogative of emperors and courtesans in the ancient world and—see Mr. Arnold Bennett—

of millionaires and actresses or ballet dancers in the modern! It is to be had, but it is not for them, the unlucky ones, who can, therefore, best find compensation by identifying themselves for a few brief hours with the heroes and heroines of these super-films. The intelligentsia, the more conscious world, the world of artists and thinkers, less socially restricted in experience and accustomed to analysing this experience, have no such illusions. They believe—those who are most vitally independent and most characteristic of this age—neither in the brotherhood of man, the redemption of the world by love, nor the reality of progress. For them the voice of the people is neither the voice of God—see all the Whitmanites and other democrats!—nor the voice of sin—see all the theologians! It is simply the voice of the people, the voice of a promiscuous herd of sentient animals presently to be replaced by a fresh herd. They have no certainty of the importance of man in the universe. The earth on which they live having dwindled to a mere speck of dust in a vast cosmic system, they cannot have that touching faith in the importance of Napoleon being a republican consul rather than an imperialistic emperor which Beethoven had. They cannot seriously believe that their individual efforts are going to make any lasting impression on the universe, therefore those works of art in which the value of man's struggles with himself, his environment and his fellows are glorified, leave them cold. They cannot share the rapturous ecstasy with which Beethoven communicates to us his spiritual struggles, when to them this spiritual struggle is merely one Freudian complex struggling with another. That scepticism which is the fruit of the intelligence of Schopenhauer, Nietzsche, Remy de Gourmont, Samuel Butler, Bernard Shaw, the forerunners of Einstein and dozens of others, is now too profound to allow them to put any trust in generalisations or ideals. Therefore they fall back on the pleasure given to the senses by small, perfect works of art. Thus in music we have this rage for the early Italian, French and English composers. We get revivals of *The Beggar's Opera* and of *Figaro* and *Don Giovanni*, but not of *Fidelio*. In the fine arts, negroid and Asiatic sculpture, with its direct appeal to the physical senses, has ousted the idealising Michaelangelo from popularity. It is significant that Samuel Butler, who had musical tastes, could not tolerate Beethoven; in this respect, as in others, he was in advance of his time. But in this return to what our intelligentsia might describe as reality, can we be so sure that we have not dropped out a piece of reality? I do not think we can. I feel that it is simply a question of emphasis, and that the revolution being complete the emphasis will return again to what our past commentators have described as Beethoven's "spiritual greatness." It will return because

Beethoven's spiritual reactions were as real as my reactions to the smell of cabbage-water. But when we do return, we shall have dropped overboard a lot of romantic humbug and, be it understood, taken on board a fresh cargo—humbug that we shall all believe.

It is thought by some people that Mozart is so popular with the moderns because he is so impersonal, so objective. It is patent to all ears that Beethoven was an idealist, but, listening to Mozart, can one discover anything about the man at all except that he was a genius? Sir Charles Stanford in his Interludes apparently does not believe in the sincerity of the present-day craze for Mozart. It is certainly strange that Stravinsky and Strauss—to name the most prominent figures—should write in a perfervid admiration of this composer with whom they would seem to have so little in common. Sir Charles Stanford says :

> "One of the most curious and inexplicable signs of our times has been the hero-worship of the disciples of so-called modernity for Mozart; of all the composers of the past they have chosen the very one who represents the complete antithesis of all their theories. He is always clear, always simple in all his work. He writes plenty of notes, but never a note too much, or in the wrong place. He is a master of technique, but a

greater master of concealing it. He is before all things the great economist, reaching all his effects by the slightest possible means. This admiration of him cannot but be on the lines of an absolute opposition to his principles. . . . If work is done as it is now, in Heaven's name let it be done without invoking the patronage of the cleanest composer the world ever saw."

Elsewhere Sir Charles Stanford remarks :

"Economy, of which Mozart was the greatest example, is relegated to the winds. It often does not matter what is played (in one case the wind played *Malbrook* in the middle of Strauss's *Heldenleben* without being discovered).

Now it is undoubtedly true that the works of Strauss's middle period and all the principal early works of Stravinsky show no evidence of belief in Mozartian principles. From *Tod und Verklärung* to the *Alpine Symphony* Strauss has shown a predilection for making a tremendous din cover the crude sentimentality—" gush," I might call it—of his temperament and thus betrayed the lack of fine-edged clarity to his musical perceptions. The awful banality and musical sloppiness of his songs would have made Mozart shudder. Yet, for all this, *Till Eulenspiegel* is much nearer Mozart than Beethoven, and there are passages in *Der Rosenkavalier*—and

I am told in later works—which show a Mozartian economy, though not the economy of Mozart. Stravinsky has shown in his recent work a reaction against the huge orchestras and the orgies of sound which we have " enjoyed " since Wagner, and of which Beethoven was undoubtedly the pioneer. His followers invoke the name of Mozart to obtain our blessing on this change of front. This may be merely strategy, but I believe that it springs from a sincere realisation that in music the æsthetic effect is not in direct proportion to the noise or to the number of instruments. No one with ears who has come to Mozart after much modern music can fail to realise this. Here I want to say that all modern musicians play Mozart, in my opinion, much too fast. The habit produced by modern music of listening to blocks of sound makes one unconsciously liable to dash through Mozart and pass over all the exquisite detail. In order to fasten and sharpen our attention, it is necessary to play Mozart more slowly than it was customary even to play him in his own day. But to return to our comparison, it should be plain that the inscribing of Mozart's name on the flag of the moderns has a very superficial technical justification, for it consists chiefly in a mere reaction from the huge orchestras and blatant din of recent music.

There is, however, another reason for the worship of Mozart by composers whose music seems to have nothing in common with his. It is to be found in the general character of his music, which is more abstract and less personal than that of Beethoven and appeals to a more intellectual sense than does the music of Wagner. Mozart is the real classical composer; he is in music the equivalent of Sophocles and Racine in literature. Many writers, both in music and literature, are thought to have the classical quality who are merely quiet and dull, but the real classical quality consists in extraordinary sensitiveness and delicacy of perception allied to an exceptional truthfulness and sense of proportion. There is one other attribute of the true classical writer, perhaps the most important of all—namely, directness. It is this more than any other which gives Greek art its outstanding eminence. These qualities were all combined in Mozart to a degree unknown before or after him. To apply the word " classical " to Bach is as ridiculous as to apply it to Beethoven or Wagner. We can only use it of them in the sense that they have become standard composers—composers whose greatness is universally recognised; but if we mean by " classical " the qualities of restraint, direct simplicity and truthfulness—without didacticism, sentimentality or emotional exaggeration—plus an extraordinary power of creating pure beauty, then Mozart is the only great composer to whom we can apply that epithet.

The reaction towards Mozart is part of the common reaction against romanticism and the dominating influence of temporary and evanescent moods in artistic work. The best minds of to-day are sick of the distorted egoism of which most modern art is the reflection. The reaction is so strong that even Beethoven's exuberant optimism and " will to conquer " is felt to be irritating. I believe this reaction to be essentially sound. Beethoven's genius is so great that I, like others, may be temporarily carried away by the *Ninth Symphony* and its Ode to Joy, but once I am out of the hall I think to myself : " Well, really, Beethoven's exhilaration is rather excessive." Life has corybantic moments, but to make the crowning work of one's mature artistic vision an apotheosis of a rather schoolboyish rapture is not what we expect from the world's greatest composer. Bach has three defects as compared with Mozart. He has not got Mozart's extreme sensitiveness to musical beauty, and he also lacks his directness and his sense of proportion. The modern who is consistent should damn Bach with Beethoven and Wagner as romantic swaggerers and megalomaniacs. It is on record that Mozart in later years thus criticised an air from his opera, *Die Entführung :* " At the time I wrote it I was never tired of hearing myself and did not know how to bring my work to a conclusion." It is a pity that Bach, whose fifty-three cantatas are a monument of misapplied energy, did not possess Mozart's amazing conciseness. Given space enough, anyone can make an impression ; Mozart could give you a work of individual flavour and beautiful form in a single page.

But there is another secret of which Mozart was the sole possessor which makes him so alluring to modern musicians, and this is his power of being at the same time highly expressive and completely formal, that is to say, controlled. It is miraculous that such expressiveness should have been attained without ever breaking bounds or in any way raising his voice. Mozart is the supreme master of nuance, but it is not the nuance of suggestion; nothing is ever suggested, everything is said, for Mozart was, above all, direct; but, although everything is said, it is said with such exquisite modulation that you think you have caught it all at once. There is an Adagio composed on March 19th, 1788, which for intense melancholy is not equalled by any composition I know of, but it is so perfectly proportioned, so concise and exact that it is possible for a careless listener to play it all through and get simply an impression of a perfect piece of architecture. Now this is a quality which maddens and bewitches the modern musician. The secret of it simply escapes him, yet he increasingly feels that it is the one thing worth doing. No one in music has done it with the frequency and the perfection of Mozart. How it was done is a complete mystery, and the more one studies Mozart the deeper the mystery becomes, for it all looks and sounds so transparently simple. It is the Greek simplicity once more, but there was more than one Greek artist; in music, however, there has only been one Mozart.

The golden age of music may be said to have concluded with Brahms, who died in 1897. I fix the death of Brahms as a finger-post in musical history marking the dividing of ways, not because Brahms was the " austere classicist " most encyclopædias and works of reference represent him to be, but because he was soaked in the old German religious tradition. Again, I use the word " religious " without reference to any particular creed or faith, but as signifying an emotional attitude towards life, particularly the emotional feeling that all men are brothers and that man is a spirit. This attitude has often been called the Christian attitude, but since it is not peculiar to Christianity, it is preferable to call it the religious attitude.

Bach, Beethoven, Brahms and, surprising as it may seem, even Wagner were saturated with this spirit. Bach was the most orthodox and least personal in his belief. To him man was infinitely the most important creature on this planet. In fact, it is doubtful whether he ever even contemplated the fact that man lived upon a planet and a small planet at that; certainly it was no part of his consciousness that man was the cleverest and most successful of the mammals. Historically, that conception had not yet dawned upon the world. To Bach man was the direct creation of God; he had free will, the choice of good and evil, and alone of all the creatures of this world he partook of the Divine spirit. In other words, each man was a dusty envelope, a " veil of flesh " clothing a divine soul, and was in consequence infinitely important.

Although a Lutheran Protestant brought up in the pious atmosphere of South German family life, Bach had more than a touch of genial vivacity. That he had enormous vitality needs no proof beyond his music, but there are his two wives and his numerous children as an additional testimony. There is also the fact that his eldest son, Wilhelm Friedemann, had a touch of genius, and that his second son, Carl Philip Emmanuel, was a quite exceptionally gifted musician. But vitality does not necessarily mean gaiety or vivacity; in the early Bach, however, there was a spark of gaiety, as may be seen from the complaint made by the consistory of the church at Arnstadt, that he " bewildered the congregation by many strange sounds," that his preludes were too long, and that when remonstrated with, he had made them too short, that he went to a wine-shop during the sermon, that he had not had any choir practices, and that a " strange lady " had been admitted into the choir and had been allowed to " make music."

It must be added that he was only twenty-one when this indictment was drawn up and that as he grew older he became more and more serious, until his personality became well-nigh submerged in that profound solemnity which stares at us from his portraits. This solemnity, this heavy, portentous seriousness which settled upon his genius like a cloud, was, I imagine, the result of that Protestant environment on a man of musical genius, tremendous vitality, but of little spiritual originality. It has been the custom during the last hundred years all over the civilised world to think of Bach as a great religious composer. The Protestant Churches of Europe and America, fortified by assurances from the highest professional authorities as to his purely musical genius, have united in struggling to perform some part of that cataract of cantatas and motets which flowed from Bach's pen with the " monotonous periodicity of a Sunday sermon," and on festival occasions have struggled with his John or Matthew passions or his B Minor Mass. This attitude to Bach persists to-day. It culminated in the late Sir Hubert Parry's book, which is full of such passages as :

" The cantata *Herr, wie Du willt,* is a very remarkable example of the depth of insight which is so often shown in Bach's musical interpretation of words. If superficially interpreted these particular words may be seen to be beset with pitfalls. They do indeed actually suggest an incomplete submission to the Divine will as the soul is made to express itself in the words, ' Ach ! aber ach ! wie viel lasst mich dein Wille leiden,' etc. The danger obviously is to accentuate the harshness of ' the Lord's will ' in order to enhance the credit of submission. In the text each pair of lines of the hymn relating to the Divine will is followed by a passage in which the soul in a sort of aside expresses its real opinion. Therefore, if the words were quite frankly interpreted in musical terms, they would express but a formal and superficial submission. Bach had in a sense to accept the situation which was provided for him and to write in a minor mode rather than the major, which would have expressed more frankly the loyal and unstinted submission to the will of the Supreme Being whose wisdom passes all understanding. . . . To suggest the insignificance of the human creature in relation to the Divine will, the music is at first confined to the highest part of the scale, the bass being supplied by violins and violas pizzicato."

Now, my first instinct is to translate the words, " Ach ! aber ach ! wie viel lasst mich dein Wille leiden " into an ironic " My goodness ! how much thy will lets me suffer," which is enough to show how different is the modern spirit. We

have not got in the twentieth century that calm
assurance that we know exactly what the Divine
Will demands of us which the eighteenth-century
Protestant Christians had. We—I am speaking
of people who have an inner activity of their
own, and are not mere imitators of the activity
of others, past or present—are, probably, not
even sure that there is a Divine Will, but we are
certain that any Divine Will that we can make
contact with is infinitely more complicated and
more difficult to understand than that referred
to by the authors of the words of Bach's cantatas.
But Bach set these German hymns to music
without any apparent consciousness of their
painful inadequacy as an expression of the spirit.
Parry admits that Bach's Leipzig cantatas were
in many cases less interesting than his earlier
works ; he even stumbles surprisingly near a perception of what was lacking when he suggests in
explanation that Bach was accommodating himself to the " necessity of addressing people who
had somewhat lost touch with the primitive
poetry of religion." Here several points immediately suggest themselves. First, it is not
the business of a great composer to accommodate
himself to any audience. Secondly, what Parry
so misleadingly calls the " primitive poetry of
religion " is just " religion," that is all. For
either religion is an activity of the spirit, i. e.
" poetry," or it is a perfunctory imitation of that
activity, a collection of formulæ or dogma, a

127

" mumbo-jumbo " intellectually remembered and publicly jabbered on Sundays with " monotonous periodicity."

Those Lutheran Christians were a vigorous stock; they could listen to immensely long sermons and cantatas with a dogged indifference to physical distress. This indifference to the weariness of the body may be regarded—has been regarded—as a triumph of spirit over matter, but it is just my point that their spirituality consisted of no more than this and that they imposed it intellectually upon themselves.

Their religious activity was an " imitation," and, like all imitations, materialistic; so it is noteworthy that when Bach shows some sign of life in his religious music it is when he is personally touched by some everyday human sentiment. Parry, speaking of the superiority of the St. Matthew Passion to the bulk of the cantatas, says that the theme with which the music deals is the brotherhood of man :

" It sets aside the glamour of Divine origin and appeals to men's hearts direct, to look upon the story of unsurpassable human goodness, patience, endurance, loving-kindness and suffering, to dwell upon every moment of it and set it before mankind as the highest state to which mankind can attain, redeeming humanity itself by the proof of its supreme possibilities of self-lessness, and winning the title to divinity by a life and death which surpassed all the experiences of mankind."

This, after the first sensible distinction, is a fair sample of the shallow, sentimental gush which gets written by clever men of religious instincts but of no creative religious originality. It is shallow gush because it will not stand the test of the experience which a profound mind can bring to it. We moderns will not accept complete selflessness, complete self-sacrifice as the ideal expression of the human spirit. The story which Parry sets before us as " the highest state to which mankind can attain," we will accept as an expression of a precious truth, but not as the whole truth. Now, I maintain that Bach's religious music is, from the religious point of view, shallow because it is a mere perfunctory adornment of a religion, not the expression of a fresh religious activity.

A religion is a dead religious activity, mummified and preserved as a method of spiritual life which those who have no spiritual life can imitate. In this sense alone is Bach's Church music religious. It is admirable in its perfunctory imitation, but whenever it is alive it is just expressing the ordinary feelings of human animals towards one another. But Parry was quite right in selecting Bach's " religious " music as necessarily his greatest. The point to which I have slowly been moving is that the modern reaction against the spiritual is really a reaction against the sham spiritual, against humbug. It does not in the least succeed in satisfying me with the jazz-music of Stravinsky or the sensual bravura of negro sculpture. That sort of thing can give all unprejudiced people pleasure, but only half-developed erotic women (and men) will find it satisfying. If, however, we are incapable of genuine original religious activity, if we are spiritually numb, far better enjoy what live faculties we have got than deceive ourselves with sentimentalism and moral humanitarian heroics. There is no harm in admiring Bach's Cantatas and Passions, Wagner's *Parsifal* and Puccini's *Madam Butterfly*, so long as we keep our tongue in our cheek. There is even virtue in recognising that Bach had more intellectual and emotional power than an infinite number of Puccinis and Stravinskys. But Bach a great religious composer! Oh dear, no! We have only had one great religious composer, and even he, great as he was—the greatest the world has known—was not altogether satisfactory.

DON GIOVANNI IN ENGLISH

THE production of *Don Giovanni* at the "Old Vic" by Mr. Clive Carey in Mr. Dent's new translation was a musical landmark. As was to be expected from Mr. Dent, the translation is admirable, and an English audience is for the first time now able to appreciate the merits of Lorenzo Da Ponte's libretto. Mr. Dent has kept in mind the fact that Mozart and Da Ponte treated the story of Don Juan not as a subject for moralising cant—or, as it is sometimes euphemistically expressed, religious edification—but in a comic spirit. It is true that Mozart in the music of the Statue scene strikes a different note, but it is one of those examples of Mozart's extraordinary genius that the music of this scene, though it sends a chill down one's spine, is yet absolutely in keeping with the music of the rest of the opera. It is in no way tragic, we get no sense of human suffering at all; it seems only fitting and proper that the Commendatore should invite Don Juan to supper in Hell in return for the audacious invitation Don Juan gave to the statue. The invitation is given and accepted in the spirit in which the first men to get into an aeroplane must have regarded their situation on leaving the earth. The situation is definitely comic though blood-curdling. As for the last scene—which had never been given before in England, except at private performances—anything less in the puritanical, sham-religious spirit could not be imagined than this charming exhortation addressed to the audience to "ponder well are you going to heaven or hell," or, as the original has it, "This is the end of those who do ill." The music Mozart has written to these words is absolutely expressionless. But although it is expressionless it has a certain cold beauty, and this is one of Mozart's secrets— this power of creating an expressionless beauty, which looks merely formal but is not. If Mozart had wanted to give any significance to these words he could have done it—no one better—but he did not; he ended as he began, in the comic spirit, and Mr. Dent, in my opinion, was absolutely justified in taking care to make that apparent. Some may think he has gone a little too far and underlined the comedy here and there. For example, when Donna Anna comes to after fainting at the sight of her father murdered by Don Juan, Mr. Dent makes Don Ottavio say : "She speaks again, give her a drop more brandy." At which of course, we all guffawed— except, I believe, Mr. Shaw, who for the first time in his life showed some respect for tradition. Loathing Donna Anna's sanctimonious horror at

the sudden appearance of Don Juan in her bed-
room as I do, I cannot be expected to find fault
with Mr. Dent's brandy, but I am prepared with
an argument for those degenerate people who find
Donna Anna a sympathetic character. It will
be granted, I suppose, that it would be fatal to a
comic opera if the principal character aroused in
us any strong antipathy. Well, Don Juan has
just murdered Donna Anna's father, and nothing
would be easier than for Donna Anna at this
crisis to get our sympathy to such an extent that
we could no longer contemplate Don Juan's
further adventures with the necessary detach-
ment. Mr. Dent's brandy dissolves our thicken-
ing emotions and clears our heads.

It is another matter, however, when the desire
to emphasise the comedy leads to the burlesque
singing of a Canzonetta which it seems to me
should be sung, in Don Juan's characteristically
light-hearted way it is true, but yet so subtly as
to retain its full musical value. Mr. Clive Carey,
however, consciously burlesqued *Deh, vieni alla
finestra*, and completely spoilt the music for us.
This was his only lapse from a delightfully
graceful and polished performance as Don Juan.

But at the "Old Vic" performance of *Don
Giovanni* the expectant audience is confronted
with a feeble orchestra whose virtuosity is as
near to zero as any group of well-behaved citizens accustomed to playing in public the violin,
the viola, the violoncello, and other unreliable

instruments can well be. It also has to gaze upon a set of singers whose perfection of youthful grace and beauty does not compensate for their vocal inadequacy. True they have voices. Mr. Dent and Mr. Carey have not gone so far in their restoration of the text as entirely to do away with the *singing* of those witty words which are so legibly printed upon the carefully distributed programmes. Every one of the company makes the most laudable and well-directed efforts at singing what the renowned Signor Lorenzo Da Ponte has written and what Mr. Edward J. Dent, with a command of language only second to that of the renowned Signor Da Ponte, has caused to flower again in a language no less susceptible to the insinuating graces of Court and University than the original.

There is no doubt that it is a triumph for Signor Da Ponte, for Mr. Edward J. Dent and for Mr. Clive Carey; but I happen to be a Mozart enthusiast and I dare say I am a little bit music-mad. I do not mind being entertained by Signor Da Ponte with the assistance of Mr. Edward J. Dent, and if Mozart is to be sung in English, then I am all for Mr. Dent's translation. But even if I watch the stage for the greater part of the night and take pleasure in the comedy, I like to have one ear listening all the time to that underflow in the orchestra, and I want, when the proper moments come, to forget all about the witticisms of the librettist, to close my eyes and concentrate my whole attention upon the music.

Here we come to a very difficult problem—namely, how far music is dependent upon its material expression. Just as a theme comes into a composer's mind unheard by any corporeal ear, in a purity that can never be communicated, so we desire instinctively to hear his music marred as slightly as possible by irrelevant matter. To the sensitive musical ear it is, for example, painful to hear the violin imperfectly played. To listen to a violinist whose notes are like the strokes of a pen with a hair in its nib is, for me, generally fatal to the music, however lovely it may be. It is obvious, however, that we cannot push this too far, as there is no mechanical means of reproducing music, whether through a musical instrument or through the human voice, that is always absolutely flawless. What in practice we do ask is that the instrument, the channel through which the music is conveyed to us, should by some trick or other make us forget itself. I am aware that most listeners do not ask this; they ask that the instrument should have some beauty of its own that will make them forget the music. They ask this in all the arts; that is the secret of the popularity of Caruso, of Clara Butt, of large numbers of painters and writers whose personality shuts off from the public that music which was ostensibly the reason of their interest in the artist.

Naturally, much depends upon our own mental

condition. There are times when we can hypnotise ourselves into enjoying a very imperfect performance; we are less critical, less exacting, or, perhaps, we are more receptive in one direction and less in another. The balance has been shifted a little, and that allows us to enjoy what otherwise would have remained sealed from us. Nevertheless, there still remains an ideal in which we are receptive in all directions to the highest degree known to our consciousness. This is the ideal to set before us in any musical or, indeed, other experience; for this argument does not apply only to art. It is here that Mr. Dent and Mr. Carey's production fails, but I dare say that if Mozart appeared in the flesh to reprove Mr. Dent for his exaggerated attention to Signor Da Ponte, Mr. Dent would reply in his own words: "Herr Mozart, you mistake my infinity for infidelity."

Every time I hear Mozart's music I ask myself what is the secret of its fascination. Why is it that all great musicians, whatever their temperaments, have united in extolling him, although they may never have agreed on any other point? However partial a musician may be to Beethoven, to Franck, to Bach, to Brahms, to Wagner, to Purcell, to Schumann, to Schubert, to Liszt, or to Tchaikovsky, he will at times dwell upon the defects of his particular god, but never will he do anything but praise Mozart. They have all followed Haydn, who, when asked by Mozart's father for his opinion, replied: "I must tell you before

God and as an honest man that I think your son the greatest composer I ever heard of."

One of the most striking of Mozart's qualities is his conciseness. Mozart can be trivial, formal, empty, but he never drifts, and he generally has a dry, intellectual sparkle, a definiteness which we should not be wrong in calling wit. Attwood, who was sent to him from England as a pupil, relates that Mozart would always rather play billiards than give him a lesson. Another passion of Mozart's was dancing, and his dancing must have had the same exactness and polish as his music. We are told that Mozart was small but beautifully proportioned, and that he was the soul of gaiety, although his usual expression was "serious and even melancholy." His sister-in-law declared that she "had never seen him angry," and contemporaries agree as to his "equanimity and mildness of manner." This mildness and equanimity harmonises with his intellectual formalism, and, so far we might be portraying the character of an extremely gifted intellectual, almost academic, musician. But the genius of Mozart resided in the combination of these qualities with a susceptibility, a sensuous delicacy, an extreme of sensibility, greater than any other composer has ever possessed. These qualities are often mistakenly thought to be feminine, but they are not. Just as only the hardest steel can take the finest edge, so it is the quintessence of masculinity that it is capable of such extraordinary sensitiveness. The tender delicacy of Mozart's loveliest airs is so fine, so impalpable, that it seems impossible that mortal ears could capture it. There is no swooning, no blurring, no mistiness, no languorous melting of perception into sensation, none of the sham " strength " of feminine composers like Strauss and Wagner, but always a clear purity of outline, always a maximum of expressiveness with a minimum of means.

MOZART

MR. BERNARD SHAW once remarked that nothing could be more uncharacteristic of Mozart than the portraits of the beautiful young man exhibited above his name in the world's music-shops. These portraits show Mozart as the most handsome, the most regular-featured of all great composers. These " classic " proportions seem at first sight to be peculiarly appropriate to a composer who is to-day universally admired as the classic of classics. Where else in music shall we find those qualities of serenity, limpidity, simplicity, lucidity which we concentrate in one adjective, Mozartian ? It is impossible to find a parallel to that flawless perfection. Whether we take a whole opera—such as the *Marriage of Figaro*—or a mere scrap scribbled impromptu on the page of a visitors' book—such as the Gigue written in 1789 for the Leipzig organist Engel—we are confronted with a completely finished musical composition in which there is not a superfluous bar, not a redundant or meaningless note. There is no " waste " in Mozart—no overlapping, no exaggeration, no strain, no vagueness, no distortion, no suggestion.

He is so simple that he is meaningless. His music *disappears*, like the air we breathe on a transparent day. Everybody who has really appreciated Mozart will admit that at one time or another they have felt a Mozart masterpiece as one would feel a still, bright, perfect, cloudless day. Such a day has no meaning, none of the suggestiveness, the " atmosphere," the *character* of a day of cloud, or storm, or of any day in which there is a mixture of warring elements whose significance has yet to appear. Such a day does not provoke or in the faintest degree suggest one mood rather than another. It is infinitely protean. It means just what you mean. It is intangible, immaterial— fitting your spirit like a glove. Thus, as Sir Charles Stanford has said, when you are a child Mozart speaks to you as a child—no music could be more simple, more childlike—but when you are a man you find to your astonishment that this music which seemed childlike is completely adult and masculine. At every age this pure pellucid day, this intangible transparency awaits you and envelops you in its unruffled light. *Then* suddenly there will pass through you a tremor of terror. A moment comes when that tranquillity, that perfection will take on a ghastly ambiguity. That music still suggests nothing, nothing at all, it is just infinitely ambiguous. Then you remember the phrase of a German critic who wrote of the " demoniacal clang " of Mozart. Then you look at a genuine portrait of Mozart, and instead of that smooth Praxitelean young beauty you see a straight jutting profile with a too prominent nose and an extraordinary salience of the upper lip, and for an instant you feel as if you have had a revelation. But that revelation escapes you as suddenly as it came and you are left face to face with a mask whose directness and clarity are completely baffling.

In endeavouring to explain Mozart to oneself, it is well to remember first of all that he was the most remarkable example of a child prodigy that has ever been known. He played the harpsichord in public at five years old. At seven he composed, and played on the harpsichord, the organ and the violin. In 1764, at the age of eight, after touring Europe, he came to London and played before the Royal Family; in London he published his third set of sonatas and wrote an anthem for four voices entitled *God is our Refuge*, which was presented to the British Museum. At the age of ten he wrote an oratorio which had a great success in Holland, and a year later, in Vienna, he wrote an *opéra bouffe*, *La Finta Semplica*, for the Emperor Joseph II. At fourteen he was taken to Italy by his father, and in Rome during Holy Week he went to the Sistine Chapel to hear the famous *Miserere* of Gregorio Allegri. Immediately on returning to his lodging he wrote down the *Miserere* from memory note for note. The same year he was subjected to the severest possible examination by the Bologna Accademia Filarmonica, passed it successfully and was awarded the degree of " compositore," although the regulations did not admit of any candidates under twenty years of age. This exercise is No. 86 in Köchel's catalogue and, in Professor Donald Tovey's words, is " written in the severe ecclesiastical style of the sixteenth century" and " abounds in points of ingenious imitation and device." In 1770 at the age of fourteen he wrote an opera entitled *Mitridate Re di Ponto* for La Scala of Milan. The orchestra of La Scala was at that time the largest in Europe ; Mozart directed it seated at the harpsichord as the fashion then was. The opera was received with enthusiasm and ran for twenty nights.

From the age of fourteen onwards Mozart poured forth a constant stream of compositions of all kinds. What is astonishing is that this immense early productivity seems in no way to have harmed the natural growth of his mind, for although there are pieces of Church music written before the age of fifteen which the best critics claim to rank as masterpieces, yet there is perceptible in his music a real development of his natural powers which ends only with his death.

It is suggested by some writers that the fact that Mozart acquired at the age of fourteen a technique equal to if not surpassing that of any living composer explains why he was able to pass through the critical years of adolescence from fourteen to twenty in ceaseless musical composition without straining his mind. For Mozart had to acquire the usual education, and his letters show —as later his invention in the *Seraglio* of the character of Osmin, words and all, proves—that he had great literary ability and possibly the inexhaustible fertility in language that he had in music. But Mozart's intellectual force was a quality inherent in the structure of his mind. One day the physiologists will be able to show us in a physiological generalisation Mozart's peculiar gift for form. Many writers on æsthetics think music is the most abstract of the arts, but it is certainly true that Mozart's are the purest works in music. One may speak of a movement of Mozart just as a mathematician might speak of a beautiful proposition of Euclid. Whereas in the music of most composers it is a case of content *and* structure, it is with Mozart a case of structure only, for there is no perceptible content—*ubi materia ibi geometria.* Nowhere perhaps is this more strikingly shown than in the overture to the *Marriage of Figaro.* I would suggest to the reader that he should buy the gramophone records of this overture and of Rossini's overture to the *Barber of Seville,* and compare them. The difference is astonishing. Rossini was born the year after Mozart's death; he also had the advantage of following instead of preceding Beethoven, and he was a composer of striking natural genius. But, after *Figaro,* listen to the *Barber of Seville*

overture with its alluring tunefulness over its easy
tum-ti, *tum-ti*, *tum-ti*, *tum-ti* bass, and you will
be struck with its straggling formlessness. Its
tunes are very engaging, but you can carry them
away with you and hear them mentally on a penny
whistle, a cornet or any instrument you like.
They are like bright threads in a commonplace
piece of stuff which you can pull out without com-
punction, as there is no design to spoil. But you
can do nothing of the sort with the *Figaro* overture. There are no bright threads to pull out.
There is *no* melodic content as such. You cannot
even hear the music in your memory apart from
the rush of the strings and the accents of the wood
wind. It cannot be played upon the piano. Take
away a note of it and the whole is completely
disintegrated. Nor can anyone put his hand
upon his heart and say what feeling that music
arouses in his breast. It is completely without
expression, as expression is vulgarly understood;
but the oftener you hear it the more excited you
become, the more passionate grow your assevera-
tions that there was never music like this before or
since. Its effect upon the mind is out of all proportion to its impingement on the senses. To
hear it is as though one had been present at a
miracle and had seen a mountain of matter blown
into a transparent bubble and float vanishing into
the sky. Your desire to hear that overture again
and again and again is the simple but intense desire
to see the miracle repeated. It is an astonishing

144

experience and it is an experience which only Mozart can give us.

It would be useless to attempt to explain this peculiar intellectual gift which was Mozart's in a degree that separates him from all other composers. It must just be stated and left. But there are certain facts known about Mozart which are so relevant to this point that they should be mentioned now. He was exceptionally good at dancing and playing billiards, which were his two chief pleasures. He was small, but his limbs, feet and hands were beautifully proportioned. He composed away from any musical instrument entirely in his head, and could complete the whole of a work, from the first note to the last, and then write it down—often some weeks or more later —from memory. Thus the overture to *Don Giovanni*—which was written on the night of October 28th, 1787, for the first performance of the opera in Prague on the next day, while his wife kept him awake by telling him fairy-stories —was not composed on that night but merely copied out from memory. He would often compose at meals, and while composing would take his napkin by two corners and continually fold and refold it very neatly and exactly. To me this is all extraordinarily illuminating. Conciseness— even conciseness so unparalleled and amazing as Mozart's—is not surprising in a composer who could work in this way. One also cannot but think that his invariable serenity and good temper—

L   145

upon which all who knew him have left comment—
was yet another sign of a perfect physical and
mental poise. It is on record that Mozart never
used glasses and that his eyesight was perfect at
his death, a fact which becomes significant when
one considers the strain music, and above all manuscript music such as was chiefly used in his day,
imposes. Although he may be bracketed with
Schubert as one of the two composers whose
fertility in melodic invention exceeds all others,
the listener never feels that Mozart is being swept
along the current of his own emotions as he feels
Schubert is. In listening to such works as
Schubert's *Octet* or his " Unfinished " Symphony,
one is conscious sometimes of a dissolution,
almost a liquefaction of the composer's sensibility which streams into the music like treacle.
It is this that makes Schubert's music often so
formless. The composer seems melting helplessly
away, so that we feel as if death alone could conclude the process. Yet melting, tender, exquisitely sweet as Schubert's melodies can be, they
are never in themselves sweeter or tenderer than
Mozart's, but only in their effect. They seem
sweeter because of the absence of that intel-
lectuality, that lucid precision which was so
integral a part of Mozart's mind. There are
passages in Mozart's pianoforte concertos which
are so piercing in their intense sweetness that I
have often stopped playing and laughed aloud
with excess of pleasure ; but Mozart's mental grip

never loosens; he never abandons himself to any
one sense; even at his most ecstatic moments his
mind is vigorous, alert and on the wing. It is
from this astounding elasticity that his conciseness
largely derives. Most artists are unable to tear
themselves away from their most delightful
discoveries; they linger at them and leave them
reluctantly, but not Mozart. He dives un-
erringly like a bird of prey on to his finest ideas,
and once the idea is seized he soars off again with
undiminished power.

Yet impossible as it is in Mozart's music to
separate form from content—which is his great,
his unique intellectual distinction, the quality
in which he surpasses all other composers—we
can range his forms in a hierarchy of value. The
overture to *Figaro* is perfect. There is nothing
to be altered, there is not a note we could wish
different and nobody but Mozart could have
written it; nevertheless, the overture to the
Magic Flute is a finer work. It also is perfect, but
it is artistically greater than *Figaro*. Wherein is it
greater? I believe we shall go least astray if we
make the comparison in purely quantitative terms.
The overture to the *Magic Flute* is a greater composition than the overture to *Figaro*, because
whilst form and content are equally one, whilst
" matter " has once again been turned to " form,"
more matter has been involved in the operation.
It was a bigger and more difficult bubble to blow.
It is because Mozart showed a tendency to blow

bigger and bigger bubbles that I said in the beginning of this essay that his development stopped only with his death.

I am conscious that some readers will dislike the manner in which I have put this comparison of *Figaro* with the *Magic Flute*. They will wonder why I do not use the familiar terms: *Figaro* is a comic opera, the *Magic Flute* was a more serious work. It expressed Mozart's religious feeling, his idealism, that is why, they will say, the *Magic Flute* overture is superior. Such expressions, I admit, are not without meaning but they are misleading. The world is full of music which is none the less worthless because it is "serious" or "religious." What we can say is that there is present in the music of the *Magic Flute* a quality which is not present in *Figaro* and a quality which we instinctively feel to be infinitely more precious. That "infinitely" is a concession to my own feeling. I hope it will appease the fanatical admirers of Beethoven, but my reason urges me to take it out. However, it must be recognised that Beethoven almost consistently attempted to blow bigger bubbles than Mozart. That he so frequently failed, that his bubbles so often burst instead of sailing off beautifully, as Mozart's do, into the upper regions of the mind will not prevent his admirers ranking him instead of Mozart as the greatest of all musicians. I do not really object to this very seriously, because one or two of Beethoven's biggest bubbles do float off successfully, although I confess I always watch them with anxiety, never in that utter confidence which Mozart inspires. But when we remember that Mozart died at the age of thirty-five, and reflect upon such works as *Don Giovanni*, the *Requiem*, the *Magic Flute* and much of his earlier Church music, it is permissible to believe that he would have successfully achieved bigger things.

Personally I would go farther. I very much doubt if Beethoven or any other composer has exceeded Mozart in vital energy. The last movement of Beethoven's Seventh Symphony has been called the " apotheosis of the dance," and in actual " sound and fury " it far exceeds anything Mozart ever wrote, but I do not feel there is as quick, as tense a " rush " in it as there is in the *Figaro* overture, there is only a bigger volume of noise. It is rumble of thunder compared with the flash of lightning. Nor is there in all Beethoven's great and intensely dramatic overtures anything more impressive, more dramatically effective than the use made of the opening chords in the *Magic Flute* overture ; but Mozart secures this dramatic intensity with a far greater economy of sound. He never bludgeons the senses into recognition of his powers, as so many inferior composers do, he appeals directly to the imagination.

It is not astonishing that a mind so well-balanced as Mozart's should show so great a sense of humour. In this he surpasses all other composers, and since the sense of humour is essentially intellectual, it is natural that Mozart, the most intellectual of composers, should be the greatest master of comic opera. But what is altogether unexpected is his power to make one's flesh creep. Nothing has ever been written of such truly diabolical verve as the aria for the Queen of the Night in the *Magic Flute*. It is the rarest event to find a light soprano who can sing this at all; it is certain that we shall never have it sung so as to do full justice to its startlingly cold-blooded ferocity. And yet that aria has the smooth glassy surface of a mere bit of *coloratura* virtuosity; but it is the surface of ice beneath which is a fathomless black water. This sinister ambiguity of much of Mozart's music is a quality quite apart from the more familiar power of striking the imagination which he shows in the music which announces and accompanies the entrance of the statue at the dinner-party in the last act of *Don Giovanni*. This is the most famous of Mozart's dramatic touches, and there is not a more thrilling moment than this in the whole of Wagner's *Ring*, or indeed in any opera that has ever been written. Yet I would like to insist that there is another and more troubling quality in Mozart's music. Linked with the " demoniacal clang " which is probably the result of that bareness which makes Mozart's music appear a mere rhythmical skeleton beside the work of more sensuous composers such as Brahms and Wagner (but a skeleton of electric vitality), there is a profoundly disturbing melancholy. It is never active in Mozart's work as it is frequently in the work of Tchaikovsky, in Brahms, in Chopin and even in Beethoven. It is a still, unplumbed melancholy underlying even his brightest and most vivacious movements. It is this which gives his music that ambiguity to which I have drawn attention. It would be an interesting psychological study to try to discover its meaning. It may be that Mozart's life was a profoundly unhappy one—he was certainly unfortunate in his environment, far more unfortunate than Beethoven, for he never had Beethoven's comparative financial security nor did he ever enjoy such appreciative and discriminating friends. It is certain that his extreme sensitiveness in unfavourable surroundings caused him great suffering, and it is possible that he was extremely unhappy in his love-affairs; but such in varying degree are the trials of all artists of genius, and I do not think they will account for the peculiar, all-pervading, transparent gloom of Mozart's music. I am not even sure that " gloom " and " melancholy " are the right words to use. Mozart is very mysterious—much more mysterious than Beethoven because his music seems to express much less of his human character. I believe that Mozart's personal life was a failure. In his last years he abandoned himself to frivolous gaiety. Without being dissipated he wasted his time and strength upon masked balls, dancing, feasting and idle gallantry. It is impossible to believe that he found such a life satisfactory. Why then did he pursue it? Mozart was not without that sense of spiritual life which we call religious. On the contrary, he had this sense as highly developed as his sense of humour—he was no La Rochefoucauld. The *Requiem*, the *Magic Flute*, *Don Giovanni*, the *Twelfth Mass*—to say nothing of much purely instrumental music—exist to prove it. If it were not so, Mozart would be enormously less important. But Mozart obviously lacked that quiet, steady, flaming faith which burns so intensely in Bach and Beethoven. This is the secret of that all-pervading gloom—that quiet hopelessness. I do not mean that Mozart was a child of the eighteenth century and consequently a realist and a sceptic. The true eighteenth-century man of the world is not troubled by any religious feelings at all; he entirely lacks spiritual sensibility. All men are materialists because all life is " matter," even if that " matter " resolve itself into positive and negative electricity—though God alone knows what that means! But " matter " varies in its sentient power. One piece of matter " Mr. A." can see, cannot hear, he is deaf; for him sounds do not exist; another piece of matter " Mr. B." hears but cannot see; another, " Mr. C." hears *and* sees but is colour-blind, for him colours do not exist, yet he living among the blind and deaf may easily convince himself that he misses nothing, and that these "colours" of which a few odd people talk are fantastic or sentimental illusions. This is the position of the true eighteenth-century "materialist." Mozart was not one of these; he was vividly aware of the spiritual colours of life, they were to him as concrete as heat and cold. But something else was lacking. I am conscious of it, but I do not know how to describe it. I can only point to Beethoven's Ninth Symphony and declare that I find it unmistakably present there. Mozart could not have written the last movement of that symphony. He was not capable of it. It expresses an emotion he had never felt. To describe this emotion as "joy" is utterly inadequate and ridiculous. It is a spiritual sublimity which surpasses in value all other human emotions, and which only the few supreme spirits of this earth have ever expressed. In many millions of years from now, men—if there are still men, or descendants of men, living on this planet—may be able to explain in biological terms the value of this emotion; or rather it will have become intelligible to them—as the value of the abstract feeling for justice is to-day becoming intelligible. At present it is the rare emotional possession of the few, but nothing can prevent its slowly dominating mankind. Its power is irresistible because it is latent in all men. Bach and Beethoven knew this and therefore—to use the extraordinarily apt and suggestive words of the Jacobean translators of the old Hebrew folk-tales—they "walked with God." Mozart did not. Mozart danced with the masked daughters of Vienna and wasted his spirit, not in passion or in sudden excesses of lust—which might not have harmed him, which might even have been beneficial to him—but in trivial coquetry and incessant tippling flirtations. This spiritual " faith " in which Beethoven and Bach lived is altogether different from that romantic " faith " in themselves which came into fashion for artists and men of genius in Europe at the beginning of the nineteenth century, when Napoleon began to talk about his " star " and Byron set the fashion of extravagant egoistic gestures. Bach had none of this, and in so far as Beethoven indulged in it it did him harm. Mozart was not handicapped through having lived before the invention of that comfortable padded cell of the soul, that lotos-island—the Nietzschean vanity of the superman-artist; and of all artists who have ever lived Mozart was least likely to fall a victim to such a snare. He had too penetrating an intelligence, too keen a sense of humour. No, he was deficient in an active power which Beethoven and Bach possessed and I think he was deficient in nothing else. In all else he was indeed superior to Beethoven and Bach and consequently to all others.

But now that I have put my finger on what I believe to be the radical weakness of Mozart, and have given my explanation of the melancholy of his music—namely, that Mozart had extreme spiritual sensitiveness but no spiritual faith in life (and by that I do not mean acceptance of any so-called religious faith)—I think I can give a different explanation of a point of technical interest. In Professor Donald Tovey's brilliant article on " Sonata Form " in the *Encyclopædia Britannica*, he says : " The sonata style never lost with him (Mozart) its dramatic character, but while it was capable of pathos, excitement and even vehemence, it could not concern itself with catastrophes and tragic climaxes." He then goes on to say that the G Minor Symphony shows poignant feeling but that it is not an embodiment of sad experiences. So far Professor Tovey, although writing about the " sonata form," is accusing Mozart of a lack of emotional content ; but then he continues : " In the still more profound and pathetic G Minor Quintet we see Mozart for once transcending his limits. The slow movement rises to a height not surpassed by Beethoven himself until his second period ; *an adequate finale is unattainable with Mozart's resources, and he knows it.*" Here we have an extraordinary confusion. In what way has Mozart transcended his limits in this work if the slow movement only rises to a height surpassed by Beethoven in his *second* period, and if his resources do not admit of his writing an adequate finale ? That the slow movement of the G Minor Quintet is surpassed by Beethoven in his second period I am inclined to deny. That the technical

resources of the man who wrote that wonderful
introductory allegro, that astonishing minuet,
that rich slow movement and that tragic introduction to the finale were inadequate to a satisfactory finale is to me unbelievable. That Mozart,
whose technical mastery at every point surpasses
Beethoven's in the opinion of, I should imagine,
ninety-nine per cent. of scholars, should have been
incapable of satisfactorily *concluding* an admitted
masterpiece through lack of technical resource is
completely unconvincing. What does Professor
Tovey mean? So sensitive a musician and so
brilliant a scholar can hardly be talking nonsense.
Let us examine that last movement of the G
Minor Quintet. What is wrong with it? In my
opinion, this: Mozart has written a really great
work, he has taken plenty of room, the design of
the quintet is magnificently spacious and he can
fill it. Not only has he all the technical resources
necessary—to talk of Mozart ever lacking technical
resource seems to me ludicrous—but he is in the
rich, abundant, creative mood to fill it, and so to
fill it that it strikes Professor Tovey as " profound
and pathetic "—words which he does not use
lightly. The third movement, *adagio*, is tragic
in its intensity. But what then happens? Mozart
concludes with a finale, light, sparkling and gay,
but once more masking an abyss of black melancholy. A finale that is utterly inadequate—
admitted! But why inadequate? It is not
technically inadequate. To spin that light-

hearted gossamer *allegro*, so that, after what had preceded, it should captivate and delude, not shock and disgust the listener, called for that technical skill which Mozart alone possessed. But, still, inadequate! That finale is beyond all denial inadequate. Why? Because, after the poignant, heart-breaking intensity of the slow movement, some affirmation of the soul is inexorably demanded. *Mozart could not make that affirmation.* He could not even attempt to make it. If he had attempted but had failed, *then* we could speak of inadequate resources. But he had no faith; he could not lift up his heart and sing from the bottom of that abyss; he could not stretch his wings and rise up out of it; he could only shrug his shoulders, and blow us another bubble. Therefore, and therefore only, he is not the world's greatest composer.

HOMAGE TO BEETHOVEN

A PERFORMANCE of Beethoven's Ninth Symphony was given at a recent London Symphony concert. Mr. Eugene Goossens conducted and the Bach Choir sang the choral section with phlegmatic calm. The performance was not one to be ashamed of from the ordinary conductor's point of view, but it was uninspired and unexhilarating.

It was the first time Mr. Goossens had conducted the Ninth Symphony, and it was the first time that some of Mr. Goossens' deficiencies as a conductor were revealed to me. It may be said that Mr. Goossens made his reputation with Stravinsky's *Le Sacre du Printemps*, and that he has consolidated it by his conducting of the Mozart operas for the British National Opera Company. But a very significant remark was made to me about this concert. A keen and intelligent amateur musician expressed his sympathy with Mr. Goossens for having to conduct a work which was so little likely to interest him, and later in the conversation he remarked that he had very little use for Beethoven, whereas he never tired of hearing Mozart. There is nothing

new in this, of course. Everybody interested in
music during the last twenty years has become
conscious of a gradually accelerating contempt for
Beethoven. A writer in the *Mercure de France*
not long ago wrote that any quartet by Mozart
was worth the entire works of Beethoven. The
name of Mozart is being found on everybody's lips.
Well, not everybody! A well-known young English composer once remarked in my presence that
he did not care for Mozart; but, nevertheless,
Mozart is the fashion, and it is quite evident that
Mr. Goossens gets more enjoyment from conducting Mozart than from conducting Beethoven.
He understands Mozart, whereas he does not
understand Beethoven at all.

Yet very little of Mozart's music is heard in
London. Every now and then we have an opera
season during which one or two operas are badly
performed, but how often do we hear a Mozart
Symphony, a Mozart pianoforte concerto or a
Mozart quartet? Busoni occasionally plays the
D Minor concerto, but I have never heard the
A Major concerto played, and I doubt if half-a-
dozen pianists in London know it, although one
might well claim it as one of the most beautiful
concertos ever written. There are, however, at
least half-a-dozen Mozart pianoforte concertos of
supreme excellence, but they are unknown to our
conductors or they would not choose—as Sir
Landon Ronald chose at his last Philharmonic
Society's concert—works for which there is so

little to be said, as the Rachmaninov concerto in
C Minor. But that concert of the Royal Philharmonic Society must have been one of the
dullest on record, and what that means only those
that know its record can judge. The craze,
carefully instigated by Mr. Edwin Evans, for
performing bad English music is partly responsible ; but if we ought to resign ourselves to listening to one new English work per concert in the
hope of a real discovery one day, that is no reason
why the rest of the programme should be bad.
When a pianist of Sapellnikov's rank comes to
London and is engaged by the Philharmonic
Society, the directors can easily ensure that there
shall be at least one musical treat for the audience
by choosing a really first-rate work for him to
play. How else are the old standards to be
upheld ? Those who have not heard a Busoni or
a Sapellnikov play Mozart's D Minor, A Major
and C Minor pianoforte concertos can never really
know what pianoforte playing is. Any fool can
play Rachmaninov—most of them do ! Mr.
Moiseiwitsch has all the appearance of a first-class
pianist in concertos by Tcherepnin and Rachmaninov, but he would be exposing his reputation to serious risks if he played Mozart, as his
occasional attempts at playing Beethoven have
shown.

So it was easy for Mr. Eugene Goossens to
impress us when he conducted Stravinsky's *Le
Sacre du Printemps*, which, although a far more

interesting work than any of Rachmaninov's pianistic melodramas, is still too fresh for us to be critical of its rendering. But if you ask me whether I consider it as original and powerful a work as the Ninth Symphony I should reply " No " ! What would Mr. Goossens say ? Well, Mr. Goossens would either equivocate or he would be in favour of Stravinsky, and he would have with him the great majority of our younger musicians. There is no need for me to say that this is sound and healthy ; it is just normal and natural, and if Stravinsky were in need of a hearing I should be on that side too, but Stravinsky has " arrived " ; what he writes is listened to with respect.

I have always been chary of writing about Beethoven. I have never mentioned him except casually and always, I think, in connection with Wagner. Wagner was a great admirer of Beethoven's music, especially of the Ninth Symphony. He remarks on the extraordinarily uncanny effect the opening fifths of the first movement always had on him, and this symphony obviously impressed him more than any other music he ever heard. Yet it is due to Wagner more than anyone else if to-day Beethoven fails to impress us, for Wagner had a genius for effect which no musician before or since has ever equalled. It is just this gift which Beethoven seems to lack. Beethoven was a fumbler. His music is full of stammers, stutters and groans, and often he suddenly takes a short cut and makes some perfectly naïve and childish bid for effect. Never was there so great a genius with so little theatrical sense. Wagner was a consummate actor. Once in his early days in Paris, after a long day chasing the streets in search of food and money, he mounted a table and delivered an oration in favour of emigration to South America and aroused his listeners to frantic enthusiasm. He was a darling of the gods, who had showered upon him almost every gift that a man can have. In fact, Wagner was so gifted that we are always tempted to do him the injustice of thinking him superficial.

Wagner, however, was great enough to appreciate Beethoven; few of us are. For Beethoven's greatness—now that Wagner and his successors have obscured his technical innovations—is wholly conceptual. Yet it might be argued that technically there is a greater gap between Mozart and Beethoven than between Beethoven and Wagner. It was always rather a struggle with Beethoven; he had to hack and hew his path, and it was a thorny, uneven and irregular path, not the grand, illuminated, asphalted avenue down which Wagner marched with his ten horns and six trombones. When I was last in Germany I saw in a prospectus of the *Drei Masken Verlag* part of a facsimile of the *Meistersinger* score. It was one of the most beautiful manuscripts I have ever seen. There was not a blot or an erasure, and it was as legible as print. I vainly tried to find out whether the manuscript was not a fair copy made by Wagner from his original draft, for I could not believe that what I saw could possibly be the original. However, we know that all the completed manuscripts of Beethoven's works extant are *not* first drafts, for Beethoven sweated blood in writing and re-writing—to say nothing of making innumerable first sketches in his notebooks. Yet Beethoven's final completed manuscripts are a mass of blottings out, scratchings, alterations and additions, witnessing only too vividly to the painfully difficult process composition was to him.

In spite of all this labour many of Beethoven's effects are woefully inadequate. The prestissimo conclusion to the last (choral) movement of the Ninth Symphony, for example, is almost ludicrous in its effect. But it is not so ludicrous when played on the piano as when it is thundered out by the orchestra in unison, and it is not ludicrous at all in the imagination, for I maintain, in spite of the opinions of certain critics, that there is nothing cheap in the *idea*. It is the application of it that is all wrong, and how far this and other mistakes are due to Beethoven's deafness is a question that has never been investigated. Nevertheless, Beethoven could not build up a concluding climax on the grand scale. The Fifth Symphony is as great a failure in this respect as the Ninth. Beethoven's music is like a series of shorthand notes intended as sign-posts leading into an elysium of the mind. Wagner's is a concrete Venusberg on earth. Yet these are minor matters when compared with the actual value of the ideas in Beethoven's work. In conception the Ninth Symphony is stupendous. Its execution does not fall far short for the greater part of the work. Who else in music could have written that first movement, that astonishing *scherzo* and that extraordinarily beautiful and wonderfully-woven *adagio*. It must also be remembered that Beethoven could occasionally write a work that flowed as smoothly and inevitably as a score by Mozart. Take the Fourth Symphony, for example. You cannot match that for lyrical spontaneity outside Schubert and Mozart. Then there is the Arietta from the Opus 111 Sonata in C Major. If there is a more flawless or more beautiful example of musical form I do not know it. These are not the only examples. But when we have said this, when we have admitted that Beethoven occasionally brought off a work that was as *musically* spontaneous and perfect as Mozart, and as " big " and effective as Wagner, we are left with something still to say, something that we cannot say about either Mozart or Wagner, who are in my opinion the two supreme examples of musical genius.

What is this " something " ? I will admit I do not pretend to be able to define it. I can only suggest that it is a quality *which does not exist*

elsewhere, and attempt to explain it by analogy.
No one who has any sensibility can listen to
Beethoven's music without realising that here is
something very far from all other music. To say
that it is as far as man is from another animal,
such as the chimpanzee, would be a pardonable
exaggeration. It may not be an exaggeration at
all. In these higher spheres the slightest difference is probably of immensely greater significance
to the future than it may seem. The difference
between the ancestors of man and the ancestors
of the apes in their first divergences was probably
imperceptible to their contemporaries, yet how
far-reaching that difference has been. In our
unimaginativeness we always assume that man
as he is is the goal of creation. Nothing could be
more fatuous! Here and there we get faint sign-
posts of the future. Beethoven was one of the
most significant. The instinct of all men and
women interested in music during the last hundred
years to believe that Beethoven was the greatest
of the world's composers is not meaningless.
What caused a man like the American Thayer—
who cared nothing for music and never once in
his three gigantic volumes of the life of Beethoven
comments on his music—to devote his lifetime
to tracking down every scrap of information about
Beethoven, travelling at his own expense all over
Europe, sifting evidence and cross-examining
witnesses? You may say it was a mere freak.
I do not believe it. You cannot read Thayer's

immense work, written in the most prosaic manner, in a style of an incredible dullness, without a feeling of awe. Significance is for the significant. There *is* something stupendous about Beethoven with which what is understood by mere musical genius is quite incommensurate. Can one read of that scene when the memorial from the greatest names of Vienna—expressing their admiration and respect for him and their desire that he should not leave the country—was presented to him without feeling that one is in the presence of some marvellous occurrence of which the actors have themselves only the faintest intuition? You will remember that Beethoven asked to be left alone and withdrew to a window in an inner room, where he sat for a long time holding the address in his hand. When he returned he said simply, in tones of deep emotion, " It is very beautiful." It is possible for an imaginative reader to catch the accent of those words. It was an accent impossible to Wagner or to Mozart or any other musician who has ever lived. In addressing Beethoven these men were addressing the human race that is to come. Open any of the great works of Beethoven—I don't mean the most flawless, the most musically successful works, but the works that are most characteristic—and you hear an utterance that is not of the world as we know it. It is of something still beyond the reach of mankind. No wonder Beethoven stammered. What is perhaps surprising is that men should have recognised that this stammering was more important than the easy magniloquence of Wagner or the beautiful limpidity of Mozart. But it is not so surprising if one reflects a little on the many mysteries of the universe.

TCHAIKOVSKY AND STRAVINSKY

IT is strange that M. Stravinsky should have thought Tchaikovsky needed championing in England, for England is the only European country outside Russia where he is popular. There are thousands of Londoners who have never heard a Brahms Symphony to whom Tchaikovsky's Casse-Noisette Suite, " 1812 " Overture, and his three last Symphonies are quite familiar. In Germany and Austria I should think Brückner and Mahler are far oftener played than Tchaikovsky. Brückner is never heard here, but one or two of Mahler's Symphonies have been performed in London. Tchaikovsky should be popular in Italy, where they have lost the power to tell a good tune from a bad one; there is an oily opulence about many of Tchaikovsky's melodies that suggests immediately Puccini, Mascagni, Woolf-Ferrari and Leoncavallo. Tchaikovsky, like Glinka, was greatly attracted to Italy, and was strongly influenced by Italian music; so was Mozart, but the difference between Mozart and Tchaikovsky is the difference between real and artificial silk or between butter and margarine. I do not think it is a friendly

168

act to Tchaikovsky to dwell over-long on his melodic gift, for it was emphatically not first-rate. It was, however, rich and copious, and I suppose the explanation of its quality is that Tchaikovsky possessed a good deal of vitality, extreme impressionability, but not a very finely adjusted nervous system, for his work is never really beautiful. His melodies always remind me of the watches in the Strand, they glitter but they are not gold.

In fairness to Tchaikovsky it must be granted that he really was inventive, spontaneous and unaffected. When he writes of his own Symphony in E Minor and Major (Op. 64), " there is something repellent, superfluous, patchy and insincere in this work which the public instinctively recognises " ; we feel we are listening to the words of a sincere but ill-balanced man. The defect of this Symphony is not that it is insincere, but that it is so much the result of mere impulse as to be nearly automatic. It is an emotional cry hardly less involuntary than the jump one might give in the middle of the night if a door were suddenly banged. Further, I think Tchaikovsky was deficient in imagination. He could not make concrete musical images charged with feeling. The Nut-cracker Suite is a good example of this, because here Tchaikovsky is obviously writing without passion, and then he is able to produce concrete musical images of a certain bright and attractive clarity, but rather empty. The great composers can produce musical images when charged with a passion that would have choked Tchaikovsky, and their images are so expressive and so beautiful in their grave purity of outline that it is the listener, not the composer, who weeps. When Tchaikovsky is moved and wants to wring our withers—and this is in five out of six of his works—he absolutely fails to touch any but the most unsophisticated of minds. Compare the most expressive of his melodies with, say, the melody with which Mozart introduces the solo piano in the last movement of the C Minor pianoforte concerto! What a difference! It is impossible for anyone to say how Mozart felt when he wrote that marvellous passage, for his feeling has disappeared into pure image, it is in perfect solution. Yet it is not a bright, cold melody empty of expression; it is, on the contrary, all expression, there is no dross, no material left in it. Tchaikovsky's melodies stick in the dross from which they were made, the emotion clings to them as a certain formless matrix clings to the bottom of a badly blown glass bottle in which the substance has not entirely disappeared into *shape*.

The Sleeping Princess, in spite of its borrowings from the Casse-Noisette Suite, does not, in my opinion, contain Tchaikovsky's best music, it is little more than bright and tuneful. When I consider the theme Tchaikovsky had to deal with—this wonderful old fairy story with its delightful symbolism—and consider how he has done nothing but provide rhythms for the dances, I feel nothing is too bad to be said about him. Even M. Stravinsky, who cares nothing for the quality of his melody, has shown more imagination in his treatment of *Petrouchka*—a story really far inferior to *The Sleeping Princess*, but set with immensely more gusto and vividness. Just imagine what a composer of real genius and passion would have made of the Awakening Scene! The delicacy, grace and infinite tenderness Mozart would have bestowed upon it, making it so fine a thing that you would scarcely have dared to breathe lest the whole scene might melt away before your eyes. But to Tchaikovsky it is just a Pantomime, and I congratulate Messrs. Bakst and Petipa on the propriety with which they respectively designed and choreographed their way through the music. What a contrast is Stravinsky's own ballet, opera, and symphonic poem: *The Nightingale*—the orchestral version of which has only been played once in London. I open the score. What a different world! How concrete, how firm and inevitable each touch! What economy of words and music, but how adequate, how moving! In a short introduction *larghetto* Stravinsky creates the atmosphere. Nothing strained, nothing laboriously manufactured, but new, original, exciting. Then the curtain rises—*paysage nocturne, au bord de la mer. La lisière d'une forêt. Au fond de la scène, le pêcheur dans sa barque.* The time alters to three-eight, the fisherman sings—a lovely folk-song melody, suffusing a calm, profound melancholy—the key changes and the time alters to five-eight. " Pale burns the moon in the sky. Calm is the sleeping wave." This is natural enchantment, as real as Shakespeare's *Midsummer Night's Dream*. The time again changes and alternates between three-four and two-four. The music becomes extremely chromatic. The fisherman is thinking of the nightingale. The time changes to three-eight.

The orchestration grows more complex and is full of secret trills. The time changes to five-eight. We are back again. " Pale burns the moon in the sky. Calm is the sleeping wave." Imperceptibly we can feel the boat rocking in the darkness under a blaze of stars. The music goes into six flats, and the time changes to four-four *andante*. Immediately the air is full of trills, descending and descending, until, after a series of modulations, suddenly *piano* but vividly, unmistakably breaks the voice of the nightingale on G flat, lifting immediately an octave *portamento*. If there is anything more beautiful in modern music than this opening scene I do not know it. The music given to the nightingale itself is of a most strange, spontaneous loveliness. I had remembered this scene on the sole occasion when I heard the opera performed, but I did not get from the opera as a whole quite the vivid, complete impression that I got from the orchestral symphonic poem. In the theatre one was somewhat distracted from the music by the scenes, whose very fantasticalness was detrimental, and, indeed, superfluous. But, listening to the symphonic poem, I became aware of how imaginative the music was. Everything is there. Stage, scenery, actors are all unnecessary. It is marvellous in its suggestive power, and it ranges from the simple but expressive folk-song of the fisherman, the strange magic of the nightingale, the fantastic pomposity and grotesqueness of the Bonze and Chinese courtiers, the appalling dead virtuosity of the mechanical nightingale from Japan, the loneliness of the sick Emperor, the motionless calm of Death with the Emperor's crown and regalia, back again to the forest by the border of the sea and the fisherman in his boat.

The music is never insincere, it is never emotional, it is always strange, vivid, aloof, but profoundly moving, and, at times, terrifying. Music so tersely imaginative has never before been written, not even by Stravinsky himself, although the chief virtue of his *Spring Rite* (*Le Sacre du Printemps*) was its imaginative power. Although the first act of *The Nightingale* was written in 1909, it is in some ways an advance on the *Spring Rite ;* it is at once more subtle, more various in expression, more economical in its means and more beautiful. The last two acts were written in 1914, after the composition of

the *Spring Rite*, but the symphonic poem is
probably still later.

It is an organic musical whole; one does not
need to know anything about the opera to understand and enjoy it, nothing could be clearer or
more compact. It is music, like the best modern
poetry, primarily appealing to the imagination,
not to the emotions or to a superficial logical
faculty.

IDEALISM leads its followers into some strange places, and the ideal of British opera is likely to lead its followers into the strangest of all. The British National Opera Company is a sort of co-operative enterprise largely made up of the wreckage of the once famous Beecham Opera Company. This company has, presumably, two ideals : one is to provide the public with British opera, by which is meant famous or notorious or infamous operatic works (by composers of no matter what nationality) Anglicised or Britonised by being sung in English—or what passes for English—by British singers. The other ideal is suggested by the word " co-operative " and means the elimination of the " star " system, by which system the payment of some fabulous—in more senses than one—sum is made to an individual singer, generally a tenor or a soprano who is expensively advertised, and on whose drawing power rather than on the merit of the performance as a whole the management relies.

Most people to-day will accept these two ideals as obviously desirable, swinging as they do from one extreme of the pendulum to the other. They will read with pleasure a recent contribution by a musical correspondent to *The Times* who exhibits his ideal for English music with the lightest of hearts. "Having patted ourselves on the back for our common sense," he says, "we will now say that we are able, like Themistocles (it is always Themistocles or Aristotle in *The Times !*), to 'improvise the thing that is wanted.' In any history of inventions the English race would not come out at the bottom of the list. (This reads like a speech by Bottomley—hear, hear !) Why do not we apply this gift to the treatment of opera ?" Ha, ha ! Why not ? Why not rehabilitate *Faust*, refurbish *Aïda*, Anglicise— or Britonise—*The Valkyrie ?* Yes, indeed, if we are true Britons this is exactly what we must do ; but there is a nasty jar coming—there always is for exuberant patriots ! *What about Shakespeare ?* Are we ready to welcome with equal enthusiasm the Americanisation of the Bard ? Will the Purcell Society (which has just sent me its admirable twenty-second volume) be willing to see twenty-five years' textual labour and scholarship cast aside by some patriotic Berliner who wants to Teutonise Purcell as ardently as our *Times* Londoner wants to Britonise Wagner ? Surely if nationalism has any value at all, this is the very negation of true nationalism, substituting for a real individuality a raging, frenzied Imperialism or Communism which seeks to put its imprint upon everything.

The way in which the British National Opera Company can be most truly national is in producing good British opera, but if it produces Italian opera, French Opera or German opera, then its duty as an artistic organisation (if that is not a contradiction in terms !) is to produce those operas intact, as they were written, in closest possible conformity with the intentions of the composer. If it does not do so it is untrue to its title of " National," for surely " national " does not apply to one nation only. In so far as the company calls itself " British," we presume it to consist of British artists, but " artist " is a more honourable, a more distinguished title than " Briton " (which may mean a blue-painted savage !), and this is recognised by the addition of the word " National," which means that this company of British artists respect and is going to take pains to show its admiration and care for the work of all other artists, whether French, German, Italian or Russian. It is, however, a strange way of showing this admiration, this care and respect for the work of other artists, if by being " national " you mean to express your intention to destroy and mutilate their work, Anglicising or Britonising what is French, German or Italian !

So far, the " Britishness " of the British National Opera Company has usually consisted in the production of sixteen non-British operas in four weeks, sung in English. This cannot be exactly described as a triumph for British music, nor would the Poet Laureate look upon it as a triumph for the English language, since, fortunately, the words were for the most part inaudible. There remain the singers, or the singer-actors. Well, the best that can be said for many of them is that they are British—artists is too flattering a term! But this company of singer-actors is to be respected. They did not follow the precepts of their *Times* adviser and Britonise *Die Walküre*. Although they sang it in English—which is, I suppose, a commercially advantageous concession to the non-musical public—they did their best with the aid of the technical staff to follow the composer's intentions, and they put up a very respectable performance. But to produce sixteen operas in four weeks is a colossal undertaking. Think of the months of preparation spent upon Mr. Nigel Playfair's *Polly*, or any ordinary musical comedy, which compared with the *Marriage of Figaro* or any average opera of the sixteen is the merest child's play. Is it any wonder that, under the circumstances, some of the B.N.O.C.'s productions are disgracefully bad—the *Seraglio*, for example, and the *Magic Flute*? On the other hand, their production of that wholly delightful opera, *Hänsel and Gretel*, and their Wagner productions are generally more creditable. But to produce sixteen operas in four weeks is not only a colossal undertaking, it is a colossal mistake. It is carrying our ability " to improvise the thing that is wanted " to absurdity. It is also extremely unfair and irritating to the public, and it does not give the good work of the B.N.O.C. a chance to get known. In one season there were only two performances of *Valkyrie*, two of *Figaro*, only one of *Siegfried*, one of the *Seraglio*, and one of *Phœbus and Pan*. For more than a week before the second performance of *Valkyrie* it was impossible to book seats, and there must have been thousands of people who were anxious to hear the Wagner and Mozart operas who were given no opportunity to do so.

There is also a certain amount of wrong casting of the rôles. Mr. Walter Hyde, for example, sings Siegmund one evening and Belmont in *Seraglio* the next ; now, a singer who could do justice to both these rôles would be a monster ; but there is sure to be miscasting in a co-operative opera company that attempts to put on sixteen operas in four weeks. The B.N.O.C. are fortunate in having Mr. Eugene Goossens frequently as conductor ; he inherits Sir Thomas Beecham's genius for improvising " the thing that is wanted " ; but he also gives me the impression that he has an artistic conscience and that he would do even better if he had more time. He does know how Mozart should be played, and it is a great pity he cannot find some way of getting more rehearsals. But what chance is there of a high standard of production in the B.N.O.C. if it continues its spasmodic attempts at putting on sixteen operas in four weeks at intervals of three or six months? I shall only begin to have faith in the possibilities of the B.N.O.C. when I see it come to Covent Garden for a season of one or two months with no more than six carefully chosen operas. But I have grave suspicions that the B.N.O.C. is not capable of the hard grind necessary for perfection. It misdoubts its capacity and feels that as there is little chance of its giving quality it must make its bid with quantity. Then if it finds that quantity, mere quantity, will not do, what are we to expect next? Why, a still stronger accent on the word "British," a still more mischievous interpretation of the word "National." We shall find the B.N.O.C. lending a co-operative ear to the malign and subversive principles of that gentleman who corresponded with *The Times*, that gentleman who, after expatiating upon the merits of the English race, and how easily we could "improvise the thing that is wanted," went on to the glorious culmination of his ideal, the notion that an opera composer need not have musical genius. "We," he says, "we have always supposed he must be a musical genius of the first order. We thought of Mozart, Beethoven and Wagner, yes, even of Mendelssohn —for the *Elijah* would make a far better opera than *Samson and Delilah*—and despaired." But, he reassures us, we need not have despaired; musical genius is in no way necessary for a composer of opera or, at any rate, of British opera. "One thing," he declares, "a composer must have." What is that, we wonder? He tells us : "A sense of the stage, a knowledge of singing and acting." "If possible," he goes on, "a composer should have sung and acted himself." Then, reflecting upon the number of people who have sung and acted themselves, he continues : "If, in addition to this, he can write pretty counterpoint, gripping harmony," it will be an advantage; but his final conclusion is that if the composer "can keep the orchestra cheerful by interesting them, so much the better."

These conclusions appeared in *The Times* under the heading "An ideal for English Music." I always knew there was something wrong with English music, and now I know what. It is too idealistic !

SAINT-SAËNS

I WONDER what the old-fashioned eugenists would say to Camille Saint-Saëns, who reached the age of eighty-six and took active part in the Liszt centenary festival at Heidelberg in 1912, but whose father died of consumption some months before his birth on October 9th, 1835. There are still quacks calling themselves eugenists who would not allow a consumptive to marry and who would relegate to themselves the right to issue certificates of fitness for parenthood according to some idiotic standard of their own—all smokers and imbibers of alcohol being naturally condemned to celibacy—but I pity the poor music critics if ever these reformers had their way, for what they call health leads in music straight to the jazz, and probably, the worse the jazz the "healthier" its author. No absolutely front-rank composer has lived to the age of C. Saint-Saëns, and, indeed, this great and serene age is perhaps—I only say perhaps—indicative of his deficiencies as a creative musician. Possibly it is not altogether fanciful to connect his evident slightness of musical vitality with his father's weakness and his own good health. Had he possessed intenser musical strength he would probably have had to pay for it with his own life. The law of the conservation of energy does not apply only to the energy of atoms, it applies to the energy of musicians, but it is mainly fanciful in its application, for we never know with what initial energy any particular musician has started. We cannot, therefore, say that a great composer must die young because a composer starting with four times the energy of C. Saint-Saëns might write with twice the energy of C. Saint-Saëns and yet live to be twice his age. On the other hand, consumption may liberate energy which would not otherwise be available for musical composition. So all we can declare definitely is that whatever the eugenists say is wrong, for they pretend to know something which is unknown and which must from its very nature still remain unknown even when science has progressed very much further than it has to-day.

Something, however, is known, and it is the quality of C. Saint-Saëns' music. It is the fashion to-day to despise it, but like most fashions it will in time go out and the public will then be free to recognise its many admirable virtues. Saint-Saëns' music has not very much melodic charm or a very individual quality. Probably the air " Mon cœur s'ouvre à ta voix " from *Samson and Delilah* is the only tune written by Saint-Saëns which the average amateur can recall, and it is not a beautiful tune ; it is, in fact, what we call "cheap." It is difficult to explain this cheapness, but we recognise that it touches a chord in us which we do not value highly—as we recognise that the involuntary flow of saliva in our mouths at the sight of a tray of cream buns is not the most exquisite sensation of which we are capable. "Mon cœur s'ouvre à ta voix" undoubtedly produces a flow of emotional saliva. This is the reason of its enormous popularity, but the opera from which it is taken can give us a pleasure superior to that, for it is admirably constructed. Compare *Samson and Delilah* with *Louise*, for example, and we shall at once discern the far greater refinement and skill of the older composer. Saint-Saëns uses the orchestra with great taste and discretion. There is none of the turgidity, the redundancy, the meaningless, noisy garrulity which in Charpentier's work is so offensive to the musician. Saint-Saëns' instrumentation is clear in colour, lucid in design and within its narrow limits expressive. He is, in other words, a genuine craftsman, who has been rigorously trained, and who turns out objects of art pleasing to connoisseurs who can appreciate skilled workmanship when they see it. He is not in the truest sense creative, he is manipulative, and that is why Wagner spoke so disparagingly of him. There is, however, a place in music for the genuine craftsman of taste, as well as for the creative artist, and there are orchestral works of Saint-Saëns—the Symphonic poems (such as

184

Le Rouet d'Omphale), some of the pianoforte concertos and the symphonies—which will continue to give pleasure to generations of musicians.

In his *Musical Memories* C. Saint-Saëns does not tell us much about himself; the composers of whom he writes are Liszt, Hadyn, Berlioz, Gluck, Massenet, Rossini, Meyerbeer and Offenbach. Perhaps the most self-revealing passage in his book is in his chapter on the organ, where he makes a strong plea for the practice of improvisation, arguing that, just as many brilliant talkers are dull writers, so there are musicians who can improvise wonderfully but whose compositions are insignificant. The organ, he says, is thought-provoking.

" As one touches the organ, the imagination is awakened, and the unforeseen rises from the depths of the unconscious. It is a world of its own, ever new, which will never be seen again, and which comes out of the darkness, as an enchanted island comes from the sea. Instead of this fairyland we too often see only some of Sebastian Bach's or Mendelssohn's pieces repeated continuously. The pieces themselves are very fine, but they belong to concerts and are entirely out of place in Church services. Furthermore, they were written for old instruments, and they apply either not at all or badly to the modern organ. . . . During the twenty years I

played the organ at the Madeleine I impro-
vised constantly, giving my fancy the widest
range. That was one of the joys of life. But
there was a tradition that I was a severe,
austere musician. The public was led to
believe that I played nothing but fugues.
So current was this belief that a young woman
about to be married begged me to play no
fugues at her wedding. Another young
woman asked me to play funeral marches.
She wanted to cry at her wedding, and as
she had no natural inclination to do so, she
counted on the organ to bring tears to her
eyes. But this case was unique. Ordinarily
they were afraid of my severity—although
this severity was tempered. One day one
of the parish vicars undertook to instruct me
on this point. He told me that the Madeleine
audiences were composed, in the main, of
wealthy people who attended the Opéra-
Comique frequently, and formed musical
tastes which ought to be respected. 'Mon-
sieur l'Abbé,' I replied, 'when I hear from
the pulpit the language of opéra-comique
I will play music appropriate to it and not
before.' "

It is curious that the names of César Franck
and Debussy are never once mentioned, but he
writes with a catholic sympathy of composers
so different as Liszt and Haydn. It is interesting

to hear him speaking of the latter composer as follows :

> " The only example of Haydn's immense work that the present generation knows are two or three symphonies, rarely and perfunctorily performed. This is the same as saying that we do not know him at all. No musician was ever more prolific or showed a greater wealth of imagination. When we examine this mine of jewels we are astonished to find at every step a gem which we would have attributed to the invention of some modern or other."

He then, after mentioning the *Seasons*, refers to Haydn's *The Seven Words of Christ on the Cross* for orchestra alone (it has appeared in other forms, but Saint-Saëns declares this to be the best) as a precious work, " delicate, touching and reserved "—originally commissioned by Cadiz Cathedral—which ought not to be neglected by modern musicians.

The most interesting chapter in the book is that entitled " Art for Art's Sake." From this chapter alone we should know that C. Saint-Saëns was a genuine musician, for he declares that the first aim of music is music and not the expression of emotion or of ideas.

> " Literature becomes art in poetry, but forsakes it in prose. Even if some of the

great prose writers rendered their prose artistic through the beauty and harmony of their periods and the picturesqueness of their expressions, still prose is not art in its real nature. . . . That is why a great poet, Sully-Prudhomme, preferred prose to verse when he wanted to write philosophically, for he feared on account of the superiority of form to substance in poetry that his ideas would not be taken seriously. . . . Because prose is far removed from art, it is unsuited to music, despite the fact that this ill-assorted union is fashionable to-day. In poetry there has been an effort to make it so artistic that form alone is considered and verse is written which is entirely without sense. But that is a fad which can't last long. Victor Hugo in his marvellous ode, ' La Lyre et la Harpe,' brings Paganism and Christianity face to face. Each speaks in turn, and the poet, in his last stanza, seems to acknowledge that both are right, but that does not prevent the ode from being a masterpiece. . . . The first prelude of Sebastian Bach's *Wohl-temperirte Klavier* expresses nothing, and yet that is one of the marvels of music. The Venus de Milo expresses nothing, and it is one of the marvels of sculpture."

Here, underneath a seeming muddle of ideas, lies the truth that music is only music when it expresses nothing but music, and poetry is only poetry when it expresses poetry and nothing else. That is what we mean by art. In so far as a poem expresses an emotional, a philosophic, a scientific, a moral or (by representation) an actual idea, it is not poetry but something else, and precisely the same is true of music. We may use poetry or music for the expression of these ideas, but what is really poetical or musical is beyond and separate from these ideas. The ideas and emotions are common to all the arts, but the music of a Mozartian melody exists in music only, and the poetry of—

> " By a lake below the mountain,
> Hangs the birch as if in glee
> The lake had flung the moon a fountain,
> She had turned it to a tree,"

cannot be expressed in any other way. It is curious that C. Saint-Saëns, who was a pure musician, did not create a finer and more abundant musical beauty.

THE FIRST DUTY OF A MUSICIAN

THE beginning of any live, intelligent interest in any art is the desire to know an artist's work in its pure, unadulterated state as it finally left the hands of its creator. In literature we have long been accustomed to have foisted upon us expurgated, amended, clarified, or otherwise bowdlerised editions of the works of prose writers and poets. Swinburne, in his " Notes on the Text of Shelley " (1869) reprinted in *Essays and Studies*, exposed to us the extraordinary aberrations of W. M. Rossetti and others, who with outstanding impudence had made or suggested a whole series of " required emendations," some, if not all, of which appeared in various editions of the poet's work. Mr. Lytton Strachey, in an article reprinted in his *Books and Characters*, reminds us of the state in which Blake's poems existed until Mr. Sampson's Oxford edition of 1905 gave us the text scrupulously reproduced from Blake's own printed, manuscript or engraved books. What Mr. Sampson did for Blake Mr. Grierson did for Donne ; but there is no end to the list of these literary saviours, without whose labours we should be completely at the mercy of commercial speculators in book-publishing, since it is impossible for everyone to examine the originals, even if he had access to them.

The same holds true of music, but the general public is at a double disadvantage here, for it never sees the greater proportion of the music it hears, and it has to rely on the good faith of conductors and performers as well as of editors. In the past this reliance on their good faith has been abused even more grossly than in literature, and editors, to say nothing of performers, have not scrupled to alter and " amend " outrageously. The voices of the purists have been raised in protest from time to time, but owing to the generally lower intellectual integrity of men of music as compared with men of letters, these protests have generally been ignored to a far greater degree. In fact, prominent musicians will take liberties with their originals to an extent that would have made the Rev. Mr. Bowdler blush ; and there are few critics with the scholarship necessary to expose them. Often these perversions are traditional, originating in the fancy of some star performer or in the stupidity, laziness or incompetence of some Kapellmeister, while succeeding generations of musicians have blindly followed in the steps of their teachers without ever having the intellectual liveliness to investigate earlier editions and the original manuscripts for themselves. Yet it cannot be insisted too strongly that it is the first duty of performers to make certain that their texts are accurate. Unfortunately, the greater proportion of musicians care only for theatrical effect. It is only when this fails to be a sufficient passport to reputation and money that they will listen to those who tell them that the public might be induced to appreciate a more intelligent interest in music. Very few virtuosos have any interest in music; what they are interested in is themselves. Music is only the means by which they display their powers to the public. They are sublimely convinced that the public goes to hear them, not to hear the music they play; and, of course, they are right. The public has very little interest in music, although it has more than they think. Even fine artists will succumb to this infatuation, this monotonous exhibiting of their abilities, generally at the expense of someone greater than themselves. Here we must be careful to discriminate. There can be no objection to a virtuoso playing a Beethoven Sonata in a way that Beethoven would never have played it, provided he plays the notes that Beethoven wrote; for, although an ideal performance of a Beethoven Sonata may be possible, this ideal will vary with everyone and would vary even with Beethoven himself from year to year and even from day to day. Provided the player sticks to the authentic text he preserves the possibility of that variety; you can only vary from something fixed and established; once you destroy your starting-point you get, not variety, but chaos, where there is no longer any variety possible.

The purists will say, for example, that harpsichord music should be played on the harpsichord and not on the pianoforte, and that Mozart's orchestral music should be played on a small Mozartian orchestra, but while agreeing that we should occasionally desire to hear music played upon the instruments for which it was intended, I suggest that it would be absurd and pedantic always to restrict us to them; for, after all, the composer does not conceive his music in the gross tones of the instruments of his day, but with an inner ear where it has an intangible purity of line and colour which is inevitably coarsened and perverted in its transmission through strings of catgut and tubes of metal. This applies to the works of the idealists or, rather, to works of ideal beauty, and not to works in which the composer has purposely used the peculiar timbre of the instruments known to him for effects of musical colour which are an essential part of his composition. In such cases if you transfer the composition to other instruments you, of course, lose either the whole of it or an important part of it.

What is altogether execrable and unpardonable is to alter a composer's notes, or his instrumentation. Interpolation is not to be excused on any ground whatsoever, and I personally feel exactly the same about cuts. The chief argument

ENGLISH SINGERS

LONDONERS do not often have the opportunity to hear real singing. But they annually have this pleasure at concerts given by Madame Elena Gerhardt at the Queen's Hall. The last time I heard her the programme was wholly filled with Schubert's cycle *Die Winterreise*. As a *lieder* singer I suppose Madame Gerhardt is unsurpassed, and she rejoices in the perfect accompanist, Miss Paula Hegner. The accompanist in the best songs has a rôle artistically equal to that of the singer, although not so technically difficult; consequently, when a singer of Madame Gerhardt's quality has an accompanist worthy of her, we touch occasionally, in a song that is masterpiece, perhaps the pinnacle of musical achievement on the interpretative plane. To those who were fortunate enough to be present at her Schubert recital I need only recall Madame Gerhardt's singing of " Wasserflut " from *Die Winterreise*. Here we got that something more than first-rate competence, that sudden spontaneous flowering, that re-creation of the song as it first floated up on to the surface of the consciousness of the composer. It is quite extraordinary what a difference there is between an occurrence of this sort and a really first-rate performance. Madame Gerhardt's singing of " Der Lindenbaum," which had preceded " Wasserflut," was absolutely first-rate and so beautiful that—the song being a particularly lovely and well-known example of Schubert's art—it provoked a storm of applause from the entire house, which up till that moment had listened with the intensest silence, not caring to interrupt the songs as they followed one another in the cycle. The effect of this applause was refreshing, its spontaneity relaxing the somewhat stiff seriousness into which the audience had contracted itself with the intention of doing justice to Madame Gerhardt and to Schubert. Everybody breathed more naturally, Madame Gerhardt smiled sympathetically, and Miss Paula Hegner—ever so little elated one felt—plunged immediately into " Wasserflut." We had just heard a first-rate performance of a beautiful song—one of the rarest of experiences—we were now to hear that extra achievement which no amount of artistic power, of technical virtuosity, of integrity can command, since it is something which *happens*, containing elements outside the control of the individual.

Madame Gerhardt gives me more pleasure than any other singer. I have heard it said that she takes almost everything too slowly. I disagree absolutely. Nearly all music nowadays is played or sung too fast for my taste. It is, of course, easier to play or to sing fast than slow. I should like to hear any of our orchestras attempt to play a Bach Suite or Concerto at half the customary pace. Or, rather, I should not like to hear it. It would be too painful. The sustained *legato* singing of Madame Gerhardt is worth all the *coloratura* of a thousand Tetrazzinis and is immensely more difficult to achieve. One might hope that the immense audiences that have listened to Madame Gerhardt will have some influence on singing in England, but it is a forlorn hope. Even assuming that the Queen's Hall had been half full of singers at each of her recitals, one may be sure that on their return to their respective homes they would be found on the next day practising worthless songs in the same bad old way. It is only here and there in an isolated heart that there burns that passion for perfection which will develop natural ability to its full capacity. In that delightful book, *A Singer's Pilgrimage*, Madame Marchesi has a great deal to say of the British student. The spirit of the British girl student, she says, is not very encouraging :

"To begin with, thoroughness is not a British quality in women. It is not trained into them from children. Knowledge also is very scant. The studies . . . are absolutely inadequate in the public schools. They learn practically nothing, and this I have experienced personally through twenty-three years. Whenever an occasion occurred in the lesson to test their general knowledge, they would utterly fail to respond. English history is hardly known, literature non-existent—so much so that they do not know even Shakespeare, and I often have to explain to the Juliets the play of *Romeo and Juliet*, to the Desdemonas the play of *Othello*, and to the Ophelias the play of *Hamlet*, as they have never even read them. Of foreign literature they are entirely ignorant, and mythology is a closed book to the average British girl. . . . The finest works of art pass in front of a British girl's mind without awaking the slightest thought or echo; the noblest expressions in a book having connection with subjects omitted from their primary education will awake their wrath. Their ignorance makes them stand in front of a closed door and they will avoid, in consequence, these things as tiresome and incomprehensible and turn to insipid, silly, cheap literature. . . . The character of the British girl has never been allowed to develop, bloom and blossom. On the one side, she has been taught to bottle up all her feelings, and on the other her imagination is given no nourishment. . . . The British woman student is lazy—let us say that terrible word, spiritually lazy—wants the easiest work, the easiest earning (one might add ' the easiest love '), is content with a small salary, with week-ends and tea-parties. . . . The ignorance of the English girl about her own health is immense. . . . I had to teach my pupils how to eat, to drink, to sleep, to clothe themselves."

I have quoted Madame Marchesi at length because this is not the theoretic assertion of a biased superficial spectator, but is the fruit of more than twenty years' practical experience. It may be true that conditions are now a little improved and that our schools are better, but I do not think anyone can deny that the charge in the main stands true to-day. Some time ago I went to see a young girl friend, about sixteen years old, who is for the moment in what I understand is one of the best convent schools in the south of England. I asked her how much piano practice she got, and she said one and a half hours a week! A well-known London musician is the music-master at this school, but what good can he do if a girl is allowed no more than an hour and a half's work a week? What took up most of the time daily was, I learned, prayers and services. In a secular school this time spent in religious exercise would, of course, be squandered on a number of other subjects, but at the convent I have no doubt they learned the Catholic Church's ritual pretty thoroughly, and that any girl who had been there for one year would for the rest of her life be able to tell you at any hour of any month what saint's day it was without referring to the calendar. That is a truly pernicious specialisation, because it is completely isolated and meaningless ; but equally meaningless is scattered, haphazard general information. English singers generally have a large repertory of bad songs, all of which they sing equally well. Their policy of not singing one song better than another is an admirable one. They attain with superb aplomb and self-satisfaction a lowest common measure of perfection. You see the same process at work in the publishing houses. " QUANTITY not QUALITY " is the motto which should be written in letters of gold (real gold out of the immense profits !) above the doorways of the most successful of them. " He is working but without hope," said a man to Swinburne of an acquaintance. " That he is working at all shows that he is hopeless," replied Swinburne. We may apply this to our indefatigable English singers and to our equally indefatigable song publishers. If only they would stop there might be some hope, but they are determined to go on. " Determined ! " No, not " determined." It is merely a bad habit.

Yet we English have an enormous reputation

on the Continent for choral singing. In France and Italy there is practically no choral singing at all, one of the chief reasons being that in the Catholic Church the congregation plays a dumb part in the service. The hymn is an Anglo-Teutonic contrivance for getting exercise in church before the Sunday dinner. I have never quite understood why hymn-singing was so popular in Germany, where the need for action of some sort is not felt so keenly as it is in this country; but I believe the German sings to relieve his feelings, just as the Englishman sings to relieve his muscles.

Sitting in church on a Sunday morning listening to the depressing reminders of the shortness of his life and the multitude of his sins, the German feels that if he sits still much longer without doing something he will weep. So it has come to pass that at convenient intervals during the service the pastor announces a hymn, and thereupon five hundred, or five thousand, Germans rise and " weep " a hymn; after that they settle down again comfortably. We do the same, only we do not weep—we yell.

Naturally, I am speaking of the north of England and the Midlands. In the south churchgoers are, as a rule, less inclined to take a vigorous part in hymn-singing. I have friends who go to the afternoon service at the Abbey occasionally, but they do not sing—much less weep or yell; they merely find their places in the hymn-book.

These are not the stuff of which choral societies are made. The backbone of our great choral societies which exist in the north of England has been the church and chapel hymn-singing congregations of the last three hundred years. The Puritans certainly owe us some recompense for all the miseries they inflicted upon us, and in these great northern choirs we have some slight artistic compensation for the æsthetic barbarity of their ancestors.

Unfortunately, here in the south we never, or very rarely, have a chance of hearing these choirs. They are purely voluntary; in many cases the members even pay a subscription to their choral societies. They consist mostly of mill-hands and factory workers, and the cost of transport and the difficulties of making the necessary arrangements for absence from work and loss of pay make it an impossible business proposition to bring these choirs to London. Of course, London has choral societies of its own : there is the Royal Choral Society, and there is—somewhere—the London Choral Society. The Royal Choral Society is noted for its periodic performances of *The Messiah*, *The Dream of Gerontius*, and *Hiawatha*. There are people who are tired of *The Messiah*. I sympathise with them. But I do not think great masterpieces of the past should be wholly dropped; it is entirely a question of proportion. We should all be willing to hear *The Messiah* once a year, for, after all, we must remember that we get Mozart as well as Handel in *The Messiah ;* but when at least one out of every six appearances of the Royal Choral Society is in *The Messiah*, it is no wonder that the very name of this Society fills our young musicians with depression.

Then another depressing fact in connection with the Royal Choral Society is that its concerts are always held at the Royal Albert Hall. The Albert Hall is the last place on earth to which anyone who cares for music ever wants to go. It is a crime against the art to perform music in such a building. It is only fit for an Armageddon of brass bands. So the Royal Choral Society is doubly damned : it is damned for its lack of initiative, its paralysing repetition of works which, however good, are not the only good choral works that have been written ; and it is damned for performing them in a building which was intended not for a temple, but for a mausoleum of music. It is also, I regret to say, trebly damned, for the Royal Choral Society sings, it is true, but it just about sings, and that is all. With our London and suburban audiences it may pass, but it would not pass with an audience accustomed to the singing of our north-country choirs.

Then there is the London Choral Society, of which I have said such hard words elsewhere that I feel reluctant to say any more. It must, however, be admitted, in fairness to the musicians who conduct these societies, that the difficulties which confront them in attempting to run a choral society in London are almost insuperable. To begin with, Londoners know nothing about singing. The majority of them have never in their lives heard any good singing. The average suburban Londoner who considers himself or herself to be " musical " has never even heard of the " Promenades." For twenty-five years Mr. Robert Newman and Sir Henry Wood have given an annual season at the Queen's Hall nightly for four to eight weeks, where the best music could be heard played by a fine orchestra under our leading English conductor ; and these concerts are still comparatively unknown. Suburbia, or rather a handful of Suburbia, may go to our West-End theatres, but you would not see in your hand that proportion of Suburbia which goes to our West-End concerts.

Even the " Promenades " audience, amounting to, say, eight thousand out of London's millions—an eight thousand which represents the cream of London's musical culture—is at such a low stage of musical education that it applauds at the " Promenades " the good, the indifferent and the positively bad singer with almost equal gusto. The fact that bad and indifferent singing can be heard at the " Promenades " speaks for itself. There are hardly any good singers in England, and the great virtue of the old

Covent Garden Opera season was that it did give us an opportunity of hearing once a year real singing from French and Italian vocalists. Now it has gone, what have we to take its place? Nothing!

SYMBOLS IN MUSIC AND LITERATURE

"THE fact that literature must always use symbols differentiates it utterly from music," says a writer in *The Times Literary Supplement*. Having made the statement he thinks himself provided with a scientific foundation for his subsequent assertions of the peculiar esoteric character of music, of its exceptional position among the arts. "Music," he says "is as independent of the world as mathematics." Let us stop as we read and get that clear in our minds : "music is as independent of the world as mathematics." We have only got to repeat any statement a sufficient number of times to feel that it is false, but the writer of this article has not finished putting his proposition on paper before a doubt insinuates itself and compels him to add : "but it cannot, like a system of geometry, ever be applied to the real world as a hypothesis." In other words music is more independent of the world than mathematics, or rather music is independent of the world, mathematics is not. Now that will strike most of us as odd. Our first thought would be that mathematics was more independent of the world than music. Did not our hearts beat when we first heard *Rule Britannia*—I mean the non-conscientious-objecting hearts? Is it a myth that generations of schoolgirls have been made to weep by Brahms?—the Andante of the F Minor sonata, for example, with its

> " Der Abend dämmert, das Mondlicht scheint
> Da sind zwei Herzen in Liebe vereint
> Und halten sich selig umfangen."

Glimmering evening, shining moonlight, hearts in love entwined! We do not seem to be so very far from the world, even *le monde où l'on s'ennuie*. Even as our tears trickle upon the imitation ivory keys—bonzoline the stuff is called—do we not feel a voice within us crying, " This will never do, pull yourself together? " Independent of the world indeed! It is not believable! But what about mathematics? Did we not get a headache when we first looked at an algebraical equation? Tears from music, headaches from mathematics. Neither seems so very remote from this world; perhaps, after all, our writer was correct in what he originally said : " music is *as* independent of the world as mathematics." But we feel that this now means neither music nor mathematics is independent of the world, whereas he meant to say exactly the contrary.

I am going to repeat that false statement of

his, " music and mathematics are independent of
the world," and I am now going to add immediately that it is true, correct, all right. I am
afraid that at this point I shall be thought
frivolous ; but I suggest that the effect of what
I have so far written is not entirely to be expressed
in logic. It is not wholly to be apprehended by
a syllogistic sense situated in the human cranium.
I imagine, I hope, that you are a little uneasy,
that you are not quite sure where you are with
me. Why ? The answer to that question is
profoundly significant. You are uneasy, you
are uncertain, you have a complex and not a
purely intellectual reaction of your consciousness to my words because I have been using
words as a musician uses sounds, not logically but
æsthetically.

Now that is the method of all creative art,
whether the medium be vibrations of sound
(music), vibrations of light (painting), or images
of vibrations of light and sound (poetry). The
ignorant imagine that all the arts are alike. They
see no great difference between a song, a story
and a picture. This is because they get the same
kind of effect from each. In the world of art
they are what certain invertebrates are in the
zoological world, there is no differentiation of
their senses ; they are, let us say, all stomach.
As soon, however, as we cultivate and develop
our senses, differentiation begins, and as a result
of differentiation we find the same individual to

be at varying levels of development according as we approach him through this or the other sense. Here is where the confusion of the arts begins.

They are no longer alike because our response to each of them is different. That is all. Actually, if I may beg the philosophic question and simply state what I believe, they are still alike, still essentially of the same nature, since they are only manifestations of one central activity—the creative æsthetic faculty—and an all-round artistic education will prove it.

In practice, however, we may find enormous differences owing to the different stages of development at which we may find the different arts, or, more concretely still, the different artists. First let us take painting, because I believe that at the moment we are further educated in our apprehension of painting than in our apprehension of music or literature. Everybody who knows anything to-day knows that it is not enough to go to a picture to be told a story, or to recognise one's birthplace. But this is how ordinary ignorant people look at pictures. Sit any Sunday afternoon in the National Gallery, and you will hear somebody say in front of a Gainsborough : " What a nice family ! look at that little girl : isn't she sweet ! " A painter once told me that he watched a family group wandering listless and dull-eyed through the gallery, glancing casually from picture to picture until suddenly one of the party, a small girl, saw a landscape and cried out: "O-oh, look, there's where Bill's hat blew off!" and immediately the eyes of the whole group brightened as they collected eagerly around this picture of a place they had visited on some club picnic.

Of course their previous boredom was due to the fact that they got nothing from the pictures but representations of objects which did not interest them. If you are shown an album of photographs of people you don't know, you have got to be either a photographer, an ethnologist or an amateur detective to take any interest in them—that is, if the people were taken naked. The addition of clothes would provide an interest for the sociologist, the dress-designer and the comic caricaturist. The addition of furniture or buildings would add a fresh range of specialists to the crowd of onlookers—in fact the only limit to the interest of any object is the intelligence of the beholder. All these interests may be purely intellectual, not æsthetic. That distinction, I hope, is clear. But let us assume that the photographer might have so posed his subject and so placed this object in his photograph—assuming it to be a nude figure—that it at once tumbled out of the world of intelligence into the world of art. No longer did we look at it as man or woman, Nordic or Mediterranean, sexually attractive or unattractive, but with a free un-utilitarian, unintellectual and—I want to emphasise this specially—unemotional vision. Of course a photographer who could do that would be a wonder, he would at once abandon photography for sculpture (and the reason for this I might be able to explain), but that it could be done is not to be doubted, for we have photographs of sculpture which to a diminished degree, but yet to some degree, give us the effect of the originals. It is in this sense that the seeming false statement that music and mathematics are independent of the world is nevertheless true?

Herein is nothing new, it is become a commonplace of art criticism, it is the truth underlying all the aberrations and errors in the writings of our best critics of painting and sculpture, from Mr. Roger Fry to Mr. Clutton Brock, but I want to take it much further. I want to suggest that the artistic medium in itself, whether vibrations of sound (music), vibrations of light (painting), or images of sensation (poetry), has no æsthetic value or meaning, and that what is true of one art—æsthetically, not practically—is true of another.

When I first enunciated my theory that there was no essential difference between music and literature—in contradistinction to the writer in *The Times*, who upheld the superiority, the other-worldliness of music to literature—I was met with various objections. The editor of a musical paper wrote thus in his weekly editorial notes :

"It is strange how the minds of some musical critics work. Here is Mr. W. J. Turner trying to disprove the statement (quoted by me from *The Times*) that 'the fact that literature must always use symbols differentiates it utterly from music.' He says: 'There is the word itself, "joy"; is not that an invention as purely abstract as the chord of C major, which consists of three notes C, E, G, just as the word consists of three letters J, O, Y. Take the letters Y, O, J, and they have of themselves no more and no less significance than the notes G, E and C have of themselves. Yet the æsthetic faculty does something with them, something mysterious and quite beyond the reach of reason.'

"Yes, Mr. Turner. What it does is to use these letters as symbols, whereas music uses the combined sounds of the three notes represented by the symbols C, E and G as an abstract invention. So the whole fabric of Mr. Turner's contention seems to fall to the ground."

I like that "seems." It is the most deceptive semblance I have ever known. What is the difference between a " symbol " and an " abstract invention "? The word "joy" is a symbol, the chord "C E G" is an abstract invention, but a symbol *is* an abstract invention—mathematical signs and musical notation are just as much symbols as letters are, so the whole of Mr. Turner's fabric stays where it was. The extraordinary confusion of mind of our musical editor and, with him, of most musicians (for I stand almost alone in my position), is further shown by his next sentence, which runs : " Why, if Mr. Turner feels like this and also thinks, as he said the other day, that the only poetry which should be set to music is bad poetry, and the only music which should be written to poetry is bad music, does not he confine himself to the art with which he is more in sympathy ? " The muddle here is quite extraordinary. First of all, I do not show more sympathy with poetry by saying only bad poetry should be set to music, than I show with music when I say conversely that only bad music should be set to poetry. Musicians and poets will one day come to see that I am right. A year or two ago, Sir Thomas Beecham's son set Shakespeare's *Merchant of Venice* to music. I said at the time that musically this was an artistic blunder. Why are people so surprised at this ? It is just as absurd to set Shakespeare to music as it would be to set a Beethoven Quartet to words. If it does not appear so absurd, it is because people in their response to literature are less æsthetically developed than in their response to music. There are reasons for this which I might expound, but I will just name one, and it is the existence of compulsory education, in letters as compared with no compulsory education in music, resulting in a lower mean response to literature. Finally, our poor unfortunate musical editor thinks that in writing about music I am being a creative musician. He actually asks me why I can't confine myself to words. Isn't this deplorable when I have never been anything else but a writer?

But here is a more intelligent objection. A friend writes to me : " I should have thought that the letter J had by itself much less significance than the sound we call C. Its position in the alphabet is arbitrary, while that of a sound in the scale is fixed." Unfortunately what my critic says it not true. Our scales are quite arbitrary. We all know that instruments can be tuned to different pitches. We all know that our modern system of Equal Temperament is deliberately artificial; that, for example, we play on the piano the same note for C sharp as for D flat, while a violinist could play two different notes if he chose. Absolute pitch itself has no absolute meaning, but depends on the relative motion of the source and the observer. This, a well-known principle in acoustics, is known as Döppler's Law. To the ape-man there were no musical sounds; all was noise, and noises produced only the crudest of reactions, such as fear when he recognised an enemy, and a sexual stimulus when he recognised the cry of his mate. I do not believe for one moment that he got any pleasure from the songs of birds. In exactly the same way to-day men and women get a sexual stimulus from the Academy portraits of soldiers or society beauties, or some other crude intellectual recognition. That is as far as their visual artistic development goes. But my friend says : " If you strike a note, I at once get some satisfaction, not, I think, from association, but because I hear a note ; if you say a letter, I get no satisfaction unless it happens to symbolise in my mind some object or idea."

Well, now, when I say the letter " J " I am also making a sound, but why is that sound less agreeable than the sound C struck on a piano? Merely because it does not possess the quality of pitch, namely, a regularity of vibration. But if my friend heard " J " spoken by a voice of beautiful quality, the timbre of that voice might give him more pleasure than the pitch of the note C. If the letter " J " were spoken by a woman he loved, it might give him still another pleasure. You cannot argue the superiority of music to literature or literature to music in this way. The pleasure my friend gets on hearing the note C struck on the pianoforte is the intellectual pleasure of distinguishing it from a noise, of recognising the regularity of its vibrations. To base music's superiority to literature upon this is ludicrous. *Xozpenfilob, pamod ablob yelponit nonsense malabdonit ibbidozil*—your pleasure on recognising the word " nonsense " amongst that crowd of letters would equally justify a claim for the superiority of literature to music.

What my friend evidently thinks is that the medium itself has an æsthetic value or meaning. I maintain that it has not, but that originally its physical individuality was its sole artistic character. Primitive man's perception of the difference between a musical sound and a noise was æsthetic only in the sense that it was the foundation of all future musical perception. But at our stage of development we can no longer call such a primitive perception æsthetic. Some people are more susceptible to sounds, some to words, some to colour and line; but these are the rudimentary intellectual and sense perceptions; the artist who gives an æsthetic satisfaction uses them to create something else, and I contend that in every art, whatever the medium, the process is still the same.

Now what is that process ? I will quote it in Pater's words : " The arts may be represented as continually struggling after the law or principle of music to a condition which music alone completely realises; and one of the chief functions of æsthetic criticism dealing with the products of art new or old is to estimate the degree in which each of these products approaches, in this sense, to musical law."

Pater perceived that each art aspired to something more than representation; he saw that it was true of painting and sculpture; more remarkably he saw that it was also true of literature; but unfortunately Pater knew nothing of music, and mistook the logic of music for this æsthetic quality, which he recognised as the goal of every art. Pater would not have admitted a treatise on logic as his ideal work of art, yet music when it is purely abstract is merely a piece of logic. There are fugues by J. S. Bach, and many other composers, that are as much a logical exercise in sound symbols as Mr. Wittgenstein's *Tractatus Logico-Philosophicus* is in word-symbols. There is not enough for the artist here. There is a meaning in it; at least, there should be, but it is not the meaning which the artist is trying to express. The artist is satisfied neither with representation, with logic, nor with sensuousness (the flavour of the medium in which he works).

Now let us return to our *Times* writer. Misled by Pater, he compares Beethoven's C Minor Symphony with a tragedy. "The tragedy," he says, "as a condition of success must make reference to our experience of life. The ostensible matter of the tragedy, the character and incidents, must not violate our conception of reality if they are to be accepted. The tragedy must be plausible. Such considerations obviously do not apply to music." This, I maintain, is quite untrue. It is absurd to think that music has no connection with reality. But I will show how the error arises. Let us return for a moment to mathematics. I am no physicist, but in the

various efforts I have made to understand a little
physics, and in particular Einstein's theory of
relativity, I have been struck by the fact that
Einstein's theory owes its existence to an observation of reality a little bit more accurate than the
observation of previous scientists. The whole
of that marvellous and seemingly quite abstract
mathematical structure which underlies his theory
is based upon observations of what actually
happens, what actually *is*, and its superiority to
the Newtonian theory depends wholly on whether
it corresponds more completely to reality than
the Newtonian theory. By reality I mean,
provisionally, the total of human consciousness.

Now it will be admitted that the area of human
consciousness dealt with by the physicist is a
distinctly limited one. Its physical basis is the
sense of touch. This is the physical basis of the
painter's art too, and of the musician's, *and of
the writer's*. Yet how different is " touch " at
one remove, when it becomes visual; at another
remove, when it becomes auditory; and at a still
further remove, when it becomes memory!
These are the three categories of the arts of painting, music and literature; and it will be recognised that, in direct contradiction to *The Times*
writer's theory, literature is a more abstract art
than either music or painting! But to what do
these differences correspond? To call one more
abstract, more remote from reality than another
is dangerously misleading if by it we are induced

to think that in such perceptions we are in an unreal world. It is untrue to say, as our *Times* writer says, that in music we live " no life that we have lived or that on this planet we could live." On the contrary, we judge, or we should judge, music just as we judge the theory of a physicist, solely by whether or not it corresponds with reality. In other words, we ask of music as we ask of a scientific theory, or of a poem, or of any work of literature : " Is it true ? "

Now I do not pretend to expect many people to understand me. What I expect of music, literature and painting is as obscure and difficult for the ordinary man who has not thought about art and has not studied music, painting and literature to grasp as it is for the man in the street to understand Einstein's theory of relativity. It really belongs to a world outside his comprehension. Yet all live minds instinctively feel their way towards the same goal, the discovery of Truth. Why we should have this instinct, this craving for something so seemingly unsubstantial, but yet so divinely beautiful and satisfying, is the mystery of the universe. I believe that to all men and women in varying degrees comes a dissatisfaction with emotional experiences which they once enjoyed. They find they have outgrown this or that pleasure, whether it derives from a work of art or from nature—and in nature I properly include men and women. This is exactly the same phenomenon as what happens to the scientist when he gradually discards the no longer satisfying Newtonian physics for the theory of relativity.

It is what makes one discard the works of Miss Ethel Dell for the works of Mrs. Virginia Woolf, the poems of Mr. John Drinkwater or Mr. Alfred Noyes for the poems of Mr. Walter de la Mare or Mr. Robert Graves; the music of Sir Edward Elgar and Mr. Rutland Boughton for the music of Stravinsky and Debussy; the painting of Sir John Lavery or Sir William Orpen for the painting of Cézanne or of Mr. Mark Gertler.

But there is one difference between the scientist and the artist which I must point out, even if I neglect others. It is this. Although the truth the artist seeks depends upon his observation of reality, it is based on a physical and psychological observation of nature (men and women, of course, being a part of nature) which is not so dependent upon mechanical contrivances as that of the scientist. The artist, unlike the astronomer, has not got to wait upon the invention of the telescope; he has only to wait upon the mental and psychical development of the human race. This moves much more slowly than the single faculty of mechanical ingenuity, therefore we do not find in art, as to some extent we do in science, that the newest are the best. Greatness, like everything else, is relative and the super-session of Newton's theory by Einstein's does not lessen the greatness of Newton.

But the large mass of literature, music and painting produced annually is dead. It is dead because it is a mere lifeless imitation of the living. It is pernicious in so far as it prevents us from contact with the superior originals. The hall-mark of all vital art is that it is a little nearer that ideal which Pater wrongly thought belonged to music by some innate birthright. But what are the signs of its approach to that ideal? They are exactly the same in music, painting and literature : originality (which means life); an absence of sentimentality (which is one of the emotions of the temporal medium); an absence of sensuousness (excessive importance of the medium); and a similar absence of mere logic (which is the pleasure of intellectual recognition). For example, the primary object of a portrait of a woman in oils should not be (1) its resemblance to other portraits, (2) its resemblance to her, (3) its unlikeness to a water-colour. In music the logic is a musical logic which it is extremely hard to make clear to the layman. In literature this logic is just telling you something rationally. Music, though Pater did not know it, is as full of echoes, of imitation, of sentimentality and of logic as literature and painting; but the finest music— like the finest literature and the finest painting, and, I would add, the finest mathematics—is freest from these excrescences and impurities. " There are," says a writer, " elegant and inelegant mathematical demonstrations, those which merely command assent and those which provide a very high degree of æsthetic satisfaction. In these latter demonstrations the mind seems to be moving with more swiftness and freedom; the whole demonstration seems to flower in a natural and spontaneous way; we have the impression of inevitability." These are the words of a mathematician, and I am not qualified to doubt their correctness, but I know that they are true of music, of painting and of literature. I will go one step further and say that they are also true of love. Few people realise that loving is also an art that begins, as every art has done, with the crudest of sensations, and develops into a higher and more complex existence. In love, in life generally, logic, sentimentality and imitation (which is insincerity) are as hateful as they are in art. (Here I will embark upon the most provocative of my theories.)

Long ago I remember writing a dramatic article for the *London Mercury*. I was writing about a musical comedy, which was unusual; but what was still more unusual was that in this musical comedy there happened to be a young actress of unusual beauty and charm. I said in the course of my article that I hoped she would be the cause of at least one broken engagement in the pit or the gallery. The editor did what probably most editors would have done, he cut out this part of my article. Perhaps he thought it frivolous, but I am afraid that he may have thought it immoral. It was, however, neither. What is wrong with the great majority of our people to-day is that they are not discriminating, not fastidious enough. Those who think this is unimportant are wrong. Nothing is more important. When I said that I hoped that, after seeing Miss Blank, one young man at least would be dissatisfied with the young woman he was going to marry, I was expressing exactly the same sort of hope that a Professor of Literature expresses when he says to a student that he hopes one day to find him preferring Euripides to Gilbert Murray. But what is wanted is a genuine perception of the difference. I know only too well that the majority of young men are brought up, are trained not to perceive the difference between one thing and another. They are instead provided with a set of precepts or judgments euphemistically called " principles " to guide them safely through life. These principles—blinkers is their better name—are so much dead matter encumbering and hindering our being. Once in reviewing a play called *Glamour* in the *Spectator*, I said that I could not believe that the heroine as depicted would ever have gone away to spend a week-end with her employer because, as she was drawn, she was too fastidious. Then I added : it is this fastidiousness which is important, not the so-called moral precepts on which fools rely. This also was cut by my editor, who, as the world goes, is broad-minded. But it should be obvious that I was taking my stand on the very highest morality—much too high, you will perhaps believe, for most people. Well, if that is true, let them go; let them do what it pleases them to do. Men and women must realise that life requires the freedom of art. We must learn to despise academic life—which is the life lived according to conventional principles—as we despise academic art. Why? Because it is dead, because it is an imitation of what has gone before, and no one must imitate, everyone must live for him or herself a unique, individual life.

The theory that art and life are separate was a necessary stage in the development of our understanding of art, and through art, of life. But my intention here is to express my feeling that what is valuable in art as in life is truth—although none of us know exactly to what it is that we must be true! We can only slowly feel along our own individual ways to it. All those who profess to be able to put into a dogma what reality is, what the meaning of the universe is, what God is, are self-declared shams and liars, or they are just very intensely stupid.

And now I want to go one step further, and then stop. The title of this essay is " Symbols in Music and Literature." I have endeavoured to express my belief that all artists deal in symbols, and that they use them æsthetically, not logically or emotionally.

If their work has æsthetic value it is because it is in some inscrutable way true to a greater reality than the facts related. In exactly the same way I believe human beings have to live true to a greater reality than the laws of their nations, the conventions of their Society, the dogmas of their religious bodies, or the facts of their animal being. In other words, everyone has got to be an artist. Those who are not are worthless æsthetically, although they may make very useful bone-manure.

ON SINGERS AND NEWSPAPERS

WHEN we had in London, singing at the Albert Hall, that excellent example of the *diva*, Madame Tetrazzini, I frankly confess I did not go to hear her, having heard her in opera at Covent Garden without being moved out of my habitual apathy towards the grand prima donna. Madame Tetrazzini had a voice of astonishing flexibility, but of no particular beauty; it was like a piece of very good elastic, it would stretch to almost any length; but the pleasure to be got out of seeing elastic stretch is soon exhausted, and one evening of Madame Tetrazzini as Lucia di Lammermoor would last me for a lifetime. There have been operatic singers with voices not only of great range and flexibility but of great beauty, and there have been others with smaller voices who were fine artists, singing with such exquisite perfection that merely to hear them sing a scale was to be thrilled, but although singers of such technical artistry have occasionally been heard during the opera seasons at Covent Garden, sometimes in minor parts, it is strange that we very rarely get any first-rate singers coming to give recitals in London. The instrumentalist has this great

227

advantage over the singer, that the modern public is more interested in instrumental than in vocal music. Modern composers as a rule do not write concertos for voice and orchestra. Strauss and other composers have written numbers of songs with orchestral accompaniments, but they remain essentially songs. Mr. Arthur Bliss has written compositions in which the voice has what is practically a prominent orchestral part, but there is no scope in these works for that display of virtuosity which is the secret of the popularity of the instrumentalist. To display virtuosity a singer has to fall back upon operatic music, and the wonderfully good taste of the modern public tends to frown upon the introduction of operatic arias in the programme of a symphony concert. The number of singers who sing this old operatic music with a virtuosity comparable to that of a Moritz Rosenthal in a pianoforte concerto has been steadily diminishing for years, but their self-esteem has not sunk with their numbers, and this, again, is a factor in their gradual elimination from the seriously musical concert. No self-respecting conductor is going to have himself and his orchestra thrust into the background as a mere adjunct to a foolish woman in a large hat who happens to have a voice like a piece of elastic, and who from her arrival to her departure from the concert platform acts as if God had produced her but had left the creation of the rest of mankind to some subordinate.

The daily Press has been largely responsible for this high altitude of the prima donna. It imagines in its millions of readers a mad craving for news—exciting sensational news, if possible, but at any rate news. It therefore, in those times when most men are acting fairly rationally —when, for example, there is only an odd man here and there murdering another—finds an alarming paucity of news and, terrified lest its readers may go where there is more news, it laps up with avidity any " story " from any press-agent and runs it. Prima donnas who have lost their jewels, tenors who have lost their wives, violinists who have lost their " Stradivarii," are welcomed by news editors with open arms. Nothing is too fatuous or silly to make good news *provided all the other newspapers will agree to run the same story*. For, mark you, the criterion of news is not—as you might innocently think— that it is new—that you alone have got it—it is that everybody has got it ; for then, and then only, is it real news. A " story " which you alone print is obviously not a genuine story, or somebody else would have had it. A moment's reflection will show why this must be so. News editors have the whole world as their prey. No news editor has ever seen a Stradivarius violin, a prima donna's pearl necklace or an operatic tenor's wife ; if he had he would know that these things never get lost. To show real discrimination a news editor would have to be omniscient. For him, truth can only be what all newspapers combine to say. Anything that only one newspaper says is either a grand scoop or it is valueless. But you cannot have grand scoops about questions of taste or matters that depend on fine judgment; you can only have a grand scoop about an earthquake or a war—something so silly that everybody can see you have not invented it.

So that quite naturally it comes about that the news editor's attitude to all news is crystallised in the question which he always puts to himself subconsciously : " Is this silly enough for everybody to print ? "   A good news editor soon comes to have a flair for news ; this flair for news is nothing but a successful submergence of your individuality into the common fatuousness of Fleet Street, so that, at any given moment, what you are printing all your brother news editors are printing also. For a news editor to have individuality would be as fatal as for a speaker to have lock-jaw ; soon his paper would be full of material that appeared nowhere else and people would at once stop taking it. " *The Daily Scream*," you would hear people saying in trams and trains, " is a hopeless paper ; it never knows what is going on." How, you will ask, can the ordinary reader judge whether a paper knows what is going on in the world, since only a mere fraction of life can come under his own observation ? Of course he cannot know, he is incapable of accurately observing even that fraction which he sees, but he refers to his friend's paper, and when he finds his friend's paper is full of the topics that fill his own paper, he goes on reading it contentedly, for he feels that he is in the stream of things—that he is not " out of it."

No serious artist can feel flattered at being made use of by the Press as a news story. Moreover, this great publicity diminishes his real audience. The musical public is crowded out of his concerts by the economic pressure of numbers and turns to the discovery of new genius, leaving its old favourite to the indiscriminating plaudits of the social mob, knowing that in time those plaudits will destroy him, pulling him down—by a law as unavoidable as the law of gravitation—to their own level. The only salvation for the artist is economic independence, and this he generally has to obtain by self-denial. He has to learn to do without, then he can snap his fingers at the Press and at the wiles of commercial and publicity agents who wish to use him merely to feather their own nests. When he is dead the news editor will find him again, but it will not matter then, for he will have given his last recital and the worms do not pay for admission.

MUSIC IN ROME IN 1828

I RECENTLY heard in Rome an excellent performance of Rossini's *William Tell*, and I was agreeably surprised to find how much I enjoyed it. The whole opera went with great verve, the choruses were better, I thought, than we are accustomed to hear in London. There was an admirable baritone, a mediocre first soprano, a second soprano in the part of Tell's son of incredible vivacity and fascination who, I learned later, was a young Sicilian new to Rome. She had a natural production and a fine voice which she was inclined to force, but she *sang*, she did not shout as the tenor did, who rarely was on any discernible note. The music is undeniably taking in its smooth rhetorical fluency. It is also more dramatically coherent than I had expected ; there is a long scene between the three male principals in the second act, for example, which is admirably sustained.

The audience was comparatively quiet. We are evidently a long way from the days when Rossini's fellow-countrymen were so touched by the maestro's art that they wept publicly and upon each other's shoulders. Stendhal, in his

Promenades dans Rome, tells us that Rossini himself once sang for the Cardinal Consalvi, and that after Rossini had been singing a few minutes "a silent tear was seen to escape from the Cardinal's eyes and run slowly down his cheek." The "silent tear" seems to have been the inevitable tribute paid to music in the early nineteenth century, and it is sometimes a little difficult for us to understand these people who wept so profusely in their drawing-rooms and who lived in the midst of a not always comic-opera brigandage. Stendhal is writing of Rome about 1828, and he relates, as an illustration of contemporary manners, how a peasant, reprimanded for being in arrears with his payment of taxes, replied to the official : "What would you, sir ; every day I go out upon the high-road with my gun, but nobody passes ; in future, however, I suppose I shall have to go out at night also." Stendhal had a passion for music inferior only to his passion for lovely women and the *beaux arts*. But his references to music are fragmentary and casual. It is a thousand pities he did not give us more detailed descriptions and criticisms of the music he heard in Rome, for he seems to have gone a good deal into society and he occasionally refers to concerts given in private houses. On November 23rd, 1828, he writes :

"We know a young Russian of noble family and very rich who, if he became poor to-morrow and bore an unknown name, would not need to make the slightest change in his manners, he is so free from affectation. . . . He gave us a delightful concert yesterday; we had the choice of pieces and asked for a new duet by Puccini. Tamburini, who is, to-day, one of the first of living singers, sang some old music at our request. Pergolesi, Buranello and the divine Cimarosa all shone in turn. Then, to include something more modern, ' *musique à dissonances savantes*,' we chose a symphony by Beethoven, but it was shockingly played. A Society lady sang really sublimely Metastasio's *Sacrifice d'Abraham*, music by Cimarosa."

On December 4th, 1828, he writes :

" Milay N., jealous of the excellent concert given by the young Russian of whom I have spoken, has given a concert of old music. Tamburini surpassed herself, she is decidedly the finest singer of the day; Rubini's voice has a tremolo, Lablache's is becoming soupy. Madame Tamburini, one of the prettiest women in Rome, sang, wonderfully, an exquisite air by Paisiello. . . . According to the Italians there is more melody in Paisiello than in all other composers put together; which is the more singular, seeing that his airs always move within one octave. The orchestra of Paisiello is almost nil; for these two reasons he never strains the voices of his singers. Rubini, who is not more than thirty, is already worn out through singing Rossini, whilst Crivelli, sublime tenor, still sings divinely at sixty-four."

It is startling to find that in 1828 Rossini was accused of ruining singers' voices. A generation later he was to be held up by the anti-Wagnerians as a model of how to write for the voice. Of course Stendhal's notion that singing Rossini could damage a voice seems to us complete nonsense, but, while recognising that Stendhal probably knew nothing about voice-production, one wonders whether the originality of Rossini's music did not impose an emotional and nervous strain upon the singer which did the mischief. No doubt people accustomed to hearing Cimarosa and other contemporary operatic composers found Rossini extraordinarily violent and exciting. Even to-day, after all the assaults upon our nerves by Strauss, Scriabin and Stravinsky, it is easy to detect a palpitating fervour in Rossini, which becomes still more noticeable if you listen to a Rossini air immediately after one by Mozart. Rossini was the first real Italian. If we think of Palestrina, Monteverde or Vittoria, or of Michael-angelo, Raphael or Titian, we do not think of them as Italians, but as Florentines, Venetians, Romans, etc.; yet, although Rossini preceded the advent of the modern Italian nation, he is as

Italian as Leoncavallo, Mascagni and Puccini. The peculiar quality of emotion characteristic of nineteenth-century Italian operatic composers may perhaps be described as " baroque," and it is curious that the baroque style should seem to have come into fashion in music so much later than its appearance in the other arts.

The composer who most excites Stendhal's admiration is Cimarosa. Of Mozart he writes very little in *Promenades dans Rome*. In one place he says : " After having disputed about Cimarosa and Mozart until one o'clock in the morning, we have then discussed the passion which renders the soul susceptible to music:" There follows a typically Stendhalian attack on the French upper classes because they affect a fashionable indifference to the feelings of the heart. A young Frenchman, he says, fears to be seen speaking more than once to the same woman. Then he adds : " Tout ce qui en Europe a plus de vanité et d'esprit que de feu dans l'âme prend les manières de penser des Français."

If Stendhal were alive to-day and were a witness of the extraordinary way in which this French fashion of thought has seized our English intellectuals and made them more French than the French themselves, he would be astonished. The result is shown in all the arts in the complete divorce of the intellectuals from the masses. The masses still reach works of art through their more immediate, more primitive feelings. The intellectuals, in the development of their intelligence, seem to have lost all *feu dans l'âme*. Consequently, their work, though often amusing, interesting even, is sterile and insignificant. Their lack of passion makes them affect to despise passion. They turn away disgusted from the works of Beethoven and Michaelangelo to admire the piquant, enormously elaborate trivialities of Busoni and Bernini. No doubt, far better the intelligence of Busoni than the stomach-pumping of the average German or English popular composer! But is nothing else possible?

We must deplore Stendhal's complete omission of the argument about Cimarosa and Mozart; but Stendhal is haunted all through this book with the fear of being found boring. He is constantly suggesting to the reader that he may like to skip a few pages, and, by this means, secures the reading of a good many historical and informative passages; but sometimes his courage fails him altogether and he says nothing. The only other reference to Mozart I have found is the following:

> "This evening we have heard the air from the *Magic Flute*, which the tenor sings just as he attempts to play the flute. This is perhaps the only good thing in the opera, but the Italians have been astonished, their eyes seemed to be saying: "Can there really be music outside Italy?"

Evidently Stendhal had never heard the *Magic Flute* nor any opera by Mozart, or he would have known better than to imagine there could only be one good air in a Mozart opera. This ignorance is really astonishing, but it astonishes us probably not quite so much as it would have astonished Stendhal if he had been told that in another hundred years his " divine " Cimarosa would be completely ignored and almost unknown, while Mozart would be in danger of receiving universal acclamation as the greatest composer who has ever lived.

Finally, let me give a list of the composers named by Stendhal in 1828 as the most famous in his time. Here they are : Buranello, il Sassone (Hasse), Martini, Anfossi and Cimarosa. Of Zingarelli, Nazolini, Frederici, Niccolini, Manfrocci, he says they are all *sans idées*; but he finds merit in Orgitani, Fiorenti, Mercadante, Caraffa and Bellini. It is depressing to study this list and to reflect that any list we are likely to draw up to-day of our contemporaries will probably contain as many names destined to rapid oblivion as Stendhal's, and that we should possibly omit altogether the one name which will interest our descendants.

MUSICAL MISSIONARIES

IN a recent number of the London *Chesterian* there was an article by a contributor from South Australia who gave some interesting details of the progress of music in that far-away country. It is to-day impossible to be beyond the reach of the benefits of civilisation. Once upon a time it was only the news of our blessed Lord Jesus Christ that was carried to the outer parts of the earth by energetic Englishmen, together with a few indispensable amenities such as trousers, skirts and hats. The inhabitants of Australia were already hardened in the possession of these blessings, so that no such evil effects followed their use there as resulted in the adjoining Melanesian islands, where the native inhabitants have been more than decimated by Christianity and Clothes. The Australians, however, are anxious to share in the musical culture of Europe and America and, like the unsuspecting Melanesian islanders, they welcome the High Priests on to their shores. " No less a celebrity than Rachmaninov himself," says our *Chesterian* correspondent, " is announced for this year." Then he adds, " a Melbourne firm is reported to have already ordered 2000 gramophone records of a certain —— in — sharp minor."

So the missionary Rachmaninov is as successful as the missionary vessel *Southern Cross*, which, according to a report by the Rev. W. J. Durrad,[1] " is one of the chief agents in the distribution of pneumonia germs " in that part of the globe. It is even doubtful whether the visit of any bishop stimulates the sale of Prayer Books and Bibles to Mr. Rachmaninov's gramophone figure, but the clerical missionaries have this advantage over musical missionaries—that their wares are more various. " Of all the evil customs introduced by civilisation, the wearing of clothes is probably the greatest," says the Rev. W. J. Durrad. Unlike most missionaries, the Rev. Mr. Durrad does not constantly refer to the natives as the heathen, but he remarks naïvely : " The Melanesians are ignorant of the real objects of clothing and seem to look on it more as a way of ornamenting the person than as anything else." I am unaware in what light Mr. Rachmaninov regards the Australians ; whether in intimate conversation as a musical pontiff he refers to them as barbarians, savages or as " heathen " ; but he may well be forgiven if, on hearing of the Melbourne firm's order of 2000 gramophone records of his prelude, he echoes the Rev. W. J. Durrad's plaint

[1] *Essays on the Depopulation of Melanesia.* Edited by W. H. R. Rivers.

and declares that the Australians seem to be ignorant of the real value of music.

Missionary propaganda is to-day a greater evil than ever. Numbers of serious-minded people apparently believe that values are objective, that goodness, beauty and truth are concrete merchandise to be parcelled out among the inhabitants of the world, something that can be shipped from London or Berlin or Paris to Honolulu or Adelaide. Few of us have fully understood the absurdity of this way of thinking. Recently I went to see the Mount Everest film—the first film I had seen for two years. There was shown a photograph of a pilgrim encountered in Tibet who walked a pace and then measured his full length on the ground. In this manner he had travelled hundreds of miles on his way to some holy man. Behind me were two London girls, and one said to the other, " Don't they send missionaries to that country ! " They were incapable of understanding that the religious exaltation got by this Tibetan was of exactly the same nature as that which they might have attained by observing a strict fast and cessation of theatre-going throughout Lent—that between the two methods there was from an ecstatic point of view nothing to choose. If this is true of religious activity it is true of artistic activity. I believe that the occupation of the missionary is one of the most idiotic ways of killing time that the ingenuity of man has ever contrived. I frankly do not believe in literary or architectural clubs, in reading circles, in outlines of science and art, or, to put my whole attitude in a phrase, in " popularising good music." I think that in order to move about comfortably in a complex society a certain knowledge of one's environment is necessary. It is, for example, necessary to be able to take a 'bus to the principal parts of London—unless you can afford a taxi, when you pay for another man's memory. It is also necessary to be able to amuse oneself, to occupy one's leisure. What should determine the manner in which you spend your leisure should be your individual taste. The sole criterion of your methods applicable by others is the effect of the way you spend your leisure on them. Here, of course, is where the missionaries and propagandists are let in. When I agitate for the performance of Brahms or Mozart, it is because I want to listen to Brahms and Mozart and not to Wagner or Liszt; but how foolish of me to expect to live my deepest æsthetic and spiritual life *in public!* I foresee the day when all public performances of music will be definitely assumed to be of a necessarily inferior character and incapable of giving any educated person pleasure. The musical man or woman will no more think of going to a public concert than to-day the literary man would think of reading *John o'*

London's Weekly or the scientist of reading the *Outline of Science*. Literary men and scientists may use those productions as a means of awakening the interest of the dawning minds of the young. Personally, I have my doubts as to their value even for that, but, then, I have my grave doubts as to the value of anything which is not a secret discovery, an isolated flowering of the human soul, alone and solitary. There is, of course, a deep-rooted, persistent desire in the human personality to communicate itself. This is at the bottom of all genuine artistic endeavour, but this communication is what happens when the artist successfully achieves a work of art. He has then objectified his desire, but if he thinks that it is now something that can be exported to the " heathen " he is mistaken. All that can happen is that some other individual human personality may here and there recognise itself in the work of art. The work of art is not something that can be swallowed like a pill and will then " cure." Even our doctors have abandoned such an illusion as to the nature of pills, yet there are still liberal-minded gentlemen who think the public can be educated by swallowing with its ears the symphonies of Mozart or Beethoven ; and only the other day I attended for a few brief moments—and then quickly departed—the opening of an exhibition by the Architecture Club, which was designed to produce good modern

buildings by enticing numbers of ladies and gentlemen to gaze at little architectural models.

Works of art, whether they be poems, symphonies or buildings, have spiritual value only
when they proceed from the individual soul
working alone. I say nothing of their value as
offices to sell stocks and shares in, or as a means
of exercising the brain, the hand and the critical
faculties. It is only when there is a complete
confusion of purpose that they cease to have any
value at all. But it is precisely this confusion of
purpose which the missionary spirit begets and
abets when begotten. The public is not invited
to learn how to build a house or how to judge the
solution of any technical problem in music, in
literature, in painting or in sculpture. It is
merely invited to gaze on these objects and be
made " whole." " Behold the Lamb of God and
thy sins are fallen from thee," states a profound
spiritual truth, but the catch is in the word
" behold ! " How can you " behold "? By
paying two shillings to hear the Ninth Symphony ?
By joining the new Architecture Club ? By
buying a copy of Wordsworth's poems ? or by
going into the British Museum to look at that
old Greek sculptor's figure of Death ? Not so !
There is no way of popularising, of making
accessible the Lamb of God. The nearer you
think you are, the further it retreats from you,
and of all guides the surest to land you finally

and irrevocably lost in a labyrinth of false images is the missionary. Therefore, I think the day may come when composers and poets will be ashamed to see their work advertised. They will produce it and those who find it will find it. Yet it may be that the best way to avoid advertisement is to let your work appear like all the others. Only a very few will know the difference.

A WORD TO MOTHERS

I ONCE received a letter from someone living in a Russian Baltic town asking me for my ideas on musical education. My correspondent wrote :

> " Tell me what you would do if you were me, that is to say, a mother who wants her children to have all that there is to have in life, which is, of course, quite usual in mothers, but who—which is, I think, a little unusual—does not by that understand (in music) that they should have ' piano lessons.' In fact, if I should be the cause of another couple of pianos in another couple of London flats, I should have a heavy conscience."

First of all, in order to reassure her, I quoted a short extract from what I once wrote on this subject :

> " The first thing to grasp is that music is an art of the ear, not of the eye. This sounds absurdly obvious, but it is no exaggeration to say that for the last hundred

years in England all children have been
taught music by the eye, and they have
been taught on that most horrible, most vile
of instruments, that King of Quacks, the
pianoforte—or, as it is popularly called, the
piano. The unfortunate child is put at the
piano, is shown a long row of black and white
notes arranged in the most puzzling order
possible, and he is then taught to connect
those strips of black and white with the
black dots and white spaces scattered over a
group of five lines on a sheet of paper.
Naturally, the first idea that would suggest
itself to an intelligent child would be that
the five black lines represented the five black
notes, and that the white spaces between the
lines represented the white spaces or notes
on the keyboard. But, as there are seven
white spaces on the keyboard and only four
white spaces between the lines of the staff,
there is clearly something wrong. From
this moment onwards he is confronted with
one puzzle after another. Everything that
he is taught is illogical, muddled and absurd,
so that ultimately he falls back on learning
in parrot fashion to connect certain marks
on paper with certain positions on the keyboard, and when he has attained to a certain
agile proficiency in this Pianoforte Pelman
system he is turned loose upon the world

as having had a musical education. Of course the poor fellow has not had even the faintest glimmerings of a musical education. He doesn't even yet know what music is."

I then went on to say that " ear training was the only true foundation to a genuine musical education." A child should be taught to distinguish infallibly every interval in the diatonic scale in every key, and then to recognise the different scales and also to recognise the wholly arbitrary selection of these scales from a welter of musical vibrations. In other words, music is an art of sounds just as literature is an art of words, and the first requirement to æsthetic enjoyment of either is a knowledge of the vocabulary, which is a perception of the meaning which consists in an infinite series of shades of difference. For example : " What would be the use of trying to teach children the difference between ' house ' and ' horse ' if they could not perceive that there was any difference in the spelling of the two words—if, to them, a ' u ' looked exactly like an ' r ' ? "

Actually we all acquire a certain amount of this knowledge in a haphazard manner as we go along. We are sent to school, we are " taught " in the most aimless and confused way ; nothing is ever made clear to us ; we simply ramble about in a jungle of confusions, picking our way as best we can. The more analytical and curious a mind the child has, the worse it fares, while those parrot-like intelligences which question nothing, want to understand nothing, *cannot* understand anything, absorb mechanically, word for word, figure for figure, all the formulæ—literary, mathematical or musical—which are put before them, spew them out again intact at examinations and earn endless laudation instead of universal execration! But such "knowledge" has had no more effect on the child's intelligence than distilled water has on the glass tubes through which it passes in a laboratory.

Teachers always make the mistake of underrating the intelligence of the young—I am speaking of the intelligent children, not of the parrots. They imagine that it is not necessary to explain, that their pupils will accept what they say, will swallow it whole without question; but more often this attitude of the teacher's is due to mistrust or ignorance. The mathematical master who insists that two parallel lines can never meet because he believes his pupils can only understand Euclid, is like a Baptist who believes in the act of immersion; to him it is not a symbol of an idea—a mortal, transient, artificial figment—but an absolute reality. And if the mathematics of Mr. Whitehead or of Einstein are wild, incomprehensible and mythical to him, he will ruthlessly and sincerely stamp upon any flickers of intelligence in his class, which rise tentatively and timorously to query the bald assertions of their teacher. Now, I believe that we should begin at the beginning with children, and by the beginning I mean that we should start with the simplest conceptions first, and by the simplest conceptions I mean the widest, most far-sweeping generalisations the human mind at its ripest has yet reached. In other words, I believe in starting children with Darwin and Einstein, not with the Reverend Mr. Snodgrass and Pendlebury's Geometry. By all means give them symbols that they can play with; give them the Euclidian Geometry and the Garden of Eden, but make these things alive by showing that they are only ideas to be synthesised with other ideas, and, above all, make it clear that, so far, we none of us know anything, but that we are all on a most exciting tour to find out.

Only a few people understand the importance of education, and, although education in this country is notoriously bad, in nothing is it so bad as in music. One of the few educational principles that the authorities have begun to see clearly is the paramount importance of teaching all the children in the country to read and write the English language. That—with an elementary knowledge of mathematics—is all that the curriculum of the elementary school should aim at, for the simple reason that an understanding of the English language is the key which will unlock all other knowledge.

But a key does not open doors of its own accord; you can put this key to knowledge in a child's hand, but you cannot make it use it to unlock those doors behind which the secrets of life lie carefully guarded. Nor is it so simple a matter as it seems at first sight to teach the English language, or, in other words, to put that key into the pupil's hands. We very quickly discover that instead of there being one key, one English language, there are—not fifty or a hundred thousand, but an infinite number of keys, and an infinite number of languages, all of which are called English.

There is, for example, the language of the Sporting Editor of the *Daily Yell*; there is the language of Miss Ethel M. Dell; there is the language of Mr. Rudyard Kipling; there is the language of the Poet Laureate, Dr. Robert Bridges—a language that would be unintelligible to the average reader of Kipling; there is the language of George Meredith, which would confuse and bewilder the reader of the serials in the *Daily Mirror*; there is the language of Henry James, which, if read aloud to any ordinary policeman, would cause him to arrest you on the spot as a lunatic.

Millions of children leave school at the age of fourteen or fifteen, and their knowledge of the

English language is so elementary that they remain cut off for the rest of their days from any knowledge deeper than that to be obtained from the news paragraph of their daily papers. Even the editorials, the short, snappy-sentenced leading articles of the modern newspaper, put an intolerable strain upon their powers of concentration and understanding.

We have to admit that, since the beginnings of education are to-day put within the reach of all, there must be some innate difference in mind which results in one child developing and another comparatively standing still. This difference may be real or it may only be apparent. For the child who, with the key put into his hand, fails to unlock the door to mathematics or to any of the sciences, or to literature, may be the very one who, given a key, could unlock all or nearly all the doors to music. This is an argument—irresistible in its implications—for a general compulsory musical education. If we are ever to have a rich and varied civilisation of the highest type, then every scrap of natural talent and individual idiosyncrasy must be made the most of and brought to its fullest fruition. The elements of music, as of art, literature, mathematics and science, must be taught at all the elementary, secondary and public schools throughout the country. It is the duty of every citizen as a potential father, and as a man desiring to live in the best of possible worlds, to see that every child in the country has the opportunity to find out what his natural powers and inclinations are —not only in order that all other men should benefit from them, but also in order that he may get the utmost possible out of himself in his lifetime.

My musical education and my mathematical education were both ruined by the stupid dogmatism of my teachers. It produced in me a sullen reaction. I decided within my child mind that these things were too uninteresting to go on with. This must be the experience of thousands of children, who only realise later the waste of their best learning years due to the incompetent folly and stupidity of their teachers. But now I hope it is becoming clear what a difficult question my correspondent put to me, and how impossible it is to answer it. Even with the best teaching children can only be guided. What finally determines their destiny is the initial energy within them, although bad teaching and bad guiding will cause an immense waste of that energy. Even the best teaching will not supply the power of understanding, which is the source of that real musical appreciation, that genuinely musical " life " which is not a trick of performing but a form of " being "—an actual " living." But the presence of great music, of that music which the finest spirits of the world by their own

253

energy of faith and passion have imposed upon the rest of mankind, is the only musical environment in which the child can develop.   And what it should develop to is a loving understanding, but an infinite scepticism of *that* music, and a desire, never to be quenched, for the music of the future.

MUSIC IN THE HOME

ONE feels moved to declare that the only place for music in the home is the bath-room. We all feel tempted to sing occasionally, and that is where we should be when the temptation seizes us. When I was a child, music in the drawing-room was the great curse of the age. It was in the declining days of Queen Victoria, when music meant *The Messiah*, *Elijah*, and Boosey Ballads. From every middle-class drawing-room throughout the land week by week went up on Sunday evening a lamentable howling that was described as sacred music. In those days the world was full of " Lost Chords " and " Holy Cities " and earnest contralto and baritones trying to find them.

Looking back and seeking to recapture that atmosphere of the nineteenth-century religiosity, one finds it incredible that people could have been so little conscious of their mental dreariness. Into what secret channels did their hidden vivacity flow? Certainly not into music! Was not Sullivan chided for wasting his gifts upon Comic Opera when he might have been writing oratorios and cantatas! And how well one knows what those oratorios and cantatas would have been! We have *The Golden Legend*, and the *In Memoriam* overture to show us what we have missed.

It is a pity that Mr. Lytton Strachey in his study of Queen Victoria did not make some inquiry into the musical taste of her family and that of the Prince Consort. It was very unfortunate that in place of the musical Tudors and Stuarts we should have been so unlucky as to get always the most unmusical of German princes. For there is little doubt that the influence of Queen Victoria and her Court was the most adverse possible. There is no need to go further in order to place the responsibility for the encouragement of the Oratorio and the Drawing-room Ballad which were England's substitute for music during the nineteenth century. In those days music was a young lady's accomplishment; every young Miss tinkled at the piano, and had a singing master who taught her to warble delicately and coyly—with the right number of well-founded protestations as to her lack of ability—the latest effort of the day's popular song-writer.

But have we progressed so very far from this? I believe we have, although the list of new songs advertised weekly by the leading publishing houses is not very reassuring. The Boosey and Chappell Ballad Concerts continue to flourish, though the stream of characterless songs flows no longer undiluted from the platform. A light orchestra and instrumentalists of real ability now vary the monotony, and it is noticeable at the "Promenades" that an ever smaller percentage of the audience waits for the second half of the programme, which used to be such an orgy of sentiment and bad singing. Nevertheless, these songs must be bought in large quantities, and presumably some unfortunate, unresisting audience has to hear them at its own fireside, or in the drawing-rooms of friends.

But, whoever the purchasers are, one never meets them nowadays. Occasionally I go to the house of some friends who, strictly speaking, are not musical, yet I find that when they go to a concert it is usually an orchestral concert, or the recital of some well-known artist at the Albert Hall on a Sunday afternoon. In this house you will find upon the piano *The Beggar's Opera*, or *Patience*, or a collection of folk-songs. I can't imagine what you would have found there twenty-five years ago. I do not believe they could ever have stood *Nazareth* and *The Holy City*, or *The Yeoman's Wedding* and *Alice, Where Art Thou?* But one never knows!

On the whole, I believe that this household is typical of a minority. Most unmusical families possess a piano. In the Dominions, I am told, everybody possesses a piano; in England nearly everybody. Ninety per cent. of the owners of pianofortes have no more than an imperceptible glimmer of musical taste. I say "imperceptible," because to any really musical person it would be imperceptible; but the theory of evolution inclines us to the *a priori* belief that some glimmer must be there. Now what do these possessors of pianofortes consume in the way of music? Well, I should say mostly dance music—fox-trots, one-steps, rag-time and waltzes innumerable! After that songs from the music-hall, revue and musical comedy. The " commanding premises " and the advertisements of publishers of cheap music witness to an enormous and sustained consumption of their wares.

I am told that the consumers of the drawing-room ballad look down on this public with an air of conscious superiority. *They* are musical; these others are a mere uneducated rabble. Living in somewhat stolid comfort at Muswell Hill and the less approachable suburbs, they are unaware that there are heights beyond them, where in a somewhat rarefied air are to be heard the songs of Schubert, Schumann, Hugo Wolf and Brahms. Truly, those heights are somewhat depopulated nowadays. There is but a scanty support for life there. One large soprano of Teutonic, Dutch, or Scandinavian extraction will consume in a single annual visit to the Æolian or the Wigmore Hall all the herbage which that region has produced in a twelvemonth. But even these visits of the *Bos femininus* are unknown to them. Still less known are the fashionable resorts among yet higher altitudes, where the intellectuals, the real intelligentsia, are gathered together listening to the songs of Debussy, Moussorgsky, Rimsky-Korsakov, and their own friends in a state of complete scepticism.

As we push our way upwards towards the highest altitudes, we are conscious of an ever-thinning population. Not only are people less numerous, but there are fewer and fewer houses, until finally we arrive at a region where there are only hotels, or where such houses as exist are indistinguishable from hotels. In these houses and hotels only the best music by the best artists is to be heard. Chamber-music by such superb musicians as the Flonzaley Quartet; violin-playing by such virtuosos as Kreisler and Heifetz; piano-playing by such stars as Josef Hofmann, Arthur Rubinstein and Moritz Rosenthal; and the music by such composers as Mozart, Bach, Beethoven, Brahms, Schumann, and a few care-fully selected, or not too carefully selected, moderns. We can hardly call performances so exquisite and professional of music so complex and sophisticated, " music in the home." We are now among the homeless, that handful of civilised people which drifts with a superb, superficial polish upon the highest plateaus of Europe. Can we say it is really musical? Can we say that here, at last, freed from the cramping and detestable influences of the private drawing-room—the drawing-room into which only the people whom one has known all one's life, and whom one detests with a detestation that is reciprocated, enter—can we say that here, in the public places of the *haut monde*, we have come at last to the really cultured, to the few who know, not from reputation, but by virtue of their own insight and sensibility, the true from the sham, the great from the mediocre, the exquisite and delicate from the mannered and finicking? Can we? No, we can't! How lamentable! How very lamentable!

Note.—The following is the kind of letter I receive whenever I write in this vein in a popular periodical:

" Sir,

" I have read your article in the *I.L.N.* about ' Music in the Home.' One wonders why on earth the *I.L.N.* (presumably) paid for it. One wonders, too, whether anyone who could write such an article ever had a home. But no wonder can exist on one point, and that is, that a person with your outlook on life should detest, as you avow you do, the people whom he has known all his life; and that, if they do not at least pity him, they should detest the miserable misanthropy you expound.

" It passes comprehension that any one should write such melancholy fudge. You remind one of the monkey who lost his tail and forthwith sought to persuade his fellows to cut off theirs.

"If possible, do quit this sombre vein—rise to something a little more cheery and helpful to humanity, or give up altogether favouring (?) us with your views. Other folks in these Georgian days still enjoy the melodies and harmonies of the Victorian age, and get from them a more companionable and happy frame of mind than yours, which is evidently, to use your own words—Lamentable! Most Lamentable!

"Yours faithfully,

"————.

"P.S.—How about Beecham's Pills?"

MUSIC IN THE NATIONAL GALLERY

IT is difficult to understand why painters, curators of picture galleries and connoisseurs of painting should be desirous of having music played in public galleries. One can quite realise that the idea appeals to musicians. They would turn every place into a concert hall if they had their way. What else do they exist for? They do not paint pictures, and possibly they cannot imagine why a number of beautiful rooms, admirably furnished (with pictures!) should be simply left for people to stroll vacantly about in. And at the public expense, too! What waste of space and time! Such an opportunity for musical propaganda ought not to be neglected. What could be more appropriate than the utilisation of those public buildings for the musical education of the people? Presumably we cannot afford a National Concert Hall, so why should there be a National Gallery? In what way are painters superior to musicians, that they should have this immense public building in the centre of London devoted solely to their art? It is obviously preposterous. Nevertheless, it is strange that the Director of the National Gallery should have recognised the undue favouritism of his art by the nation, and have made haste to redress the balance on his own initiative, for there has been no public complaint by the country's musical leaders. Not one of them has clamoured for concerts in the National Gallery, in the Tate Gallery, in the British Museum, or in the home of the Wallace Collection. Perhaps they do not know that these places exist. We have to remember that that is possible. Still, it is remarkable that the notion of turning our public galleries into concert halls should have occurred to Sir C. J. Holmes rather than to any of our musicians. But perhaps, now that he has led the way, they will follow, and we shall live to see the Queen's Hall turned into a picture gallery. Exhibitions of modern art will be held there in order to attract people to Symphony Concerts.

It will be objected that the Director of the National Gallery is not seeking in any way to turn it into a concert hall; he is merely, you may think, allowing occasional performances of music to entice people into the building and enliven the atmosphere. Some may even imagine that music will stimulate the public and put people into the right mood for looking at pictures. Those who think so will argue that it is difficult for the average man or woman to make the right approach to a picture. Something is needed to throw them out of the mechanism of their ordinary daily life : the charm of soft music, vaguely sounding as from a distance, it is argued, will effect this. It will prove the " Sesame " opening the doors of the place of pictorial art to those who have hitherto been unable to see them.

Well, this is one of those plausible but specious arguments that we are peculiarly prone to in modern life. Only our general muddle-headedness and haziness of thought enables it to gain credence for a moment. The fact is that it is impossible to listen to music and to look at pictures simultaneously if you are either really looking or really hearing. It is even doubtful whether, in merely strolling through the National Gallery and glancing casually from side to side, you would leave with a more pleasant general impression were your perambulation accompanied by music. There is a pleasure in the stillness and composure of a spacious picture gallery which is extraordinarily soothing after the restlessness and noise of a city's traffic. Music may be a divine noise, but it is a noise, and it can be extremely distracting and disturbing. It is very exhausting to listen to music, and it is very exhausting to look at pictures : the idea that it will be easier to do both these things simultaneously is at bottom a cynical conception based on the fact that by giving people the two tasks to perform at once, their failure to perform either will be hidden from them.

After all, this desire to make good things easy
is one of the most deplorable fashions of our time.
It is a part of the democratic instinct of the age,
but the theory of it is completely fallacious.
Books are written on music, on the fine arts, and
on poetry, with the avowed object of making
things easy for beginners. What they do is to
give the reader a substitute for the real thing.
Their authors wave before his eyes a white rabbit
produced from underneath a hat, but when put
into his hands it turns into a mere pocket-hand-
kerchief. All art is recognised and enjoyed by
direct perception. Some perceptions are more
subtle and complex than others. You may call
them more intellectual if you like, but the point
is that they are sensed directly as a unique
sensation, not grasped intellectually through a
logical argument. Education, as it is developed
in text-books and hand-books, merely familiarises
the reader with certain chains of argument; it
connects logically certain elementary perceptions;
and its greatest danger is that it gives the illusion
of knowledge without the reality. It fills the
reader's mind with the ideas of others—in other
words, with the dry husks of vanished perceptions.
I do not say that what the man in the street needs
is more emotion; I am no champion of mere
emotion; but I do say that he needs more perception. You do not make his perception of a
picture richer by playing music to him while he
is looking at it, and any musician will tell you that,

in order to listen to music properly, you should close your eyes. Even Wagner, who gave such elaborate settings to his operas and demanded such an amount of scenic manipulation that it has taxed the resources of the stage ever since— even he advised friends at Bayreuth not to bother about what was happening on the stage, but to listen to what was going on in the orchestra.

Therefore I think the experiment of playing music or of giving concerts in public picture galleries should not be encouraged. Either the music must be so hidden away and subordinated that it has no more effect than rain falling on the roof—in which case it cannot be expected to appeal to musicians—or it must reduce the pictures to complete æsthetic invisibility. Granted that to the majority of people music is without meaning and pictures are invisible, I would ask why the few who can see and hear should be prevented from doing either ?

Education is one of the greatest curses of the age. I am writing this from Germany. I have just been to the Cologne Picture Gallery, which is one of the dullest collections of pictures in the world, yet it contains a good deal of work that has genuine æsthetic interest. However, as I sat in the gallery I saw a party of German students —boys of about sixteen or seventeen—being conducted through the rooms by some professor. He was giving them a historical lecture, and I suddenly realised that it was merely as subject-matter for historical lectures that the majority of those pictures maintained a fictitious life. Æsthetically they had no life whatever. No one could get any direct æsthetic perception of value from them, for they were mere anecdotes, stories illustrated with a painful literality now to be studied with a literality equally painful. The historian, the antiquary, the chronicler, all found material in them for the exercise of their functions, and that was what education had produced! It had evolved an intellectual method of dodging life, of escaping from first-hand perceptions into a dry, mechanical operation of memory. This, I am sure, is all that education (I am speaking of what is called culture, not of craft training) does for the majority of the educated. It fills the mind with formulas and the mouth with *clichés*. To-day there are more people in the world than there have ever been before who know what Sonata Form means, but does that knowledge necessarily make them better listeners? Unfortunately it does not.

MUSIC IN THE CINEMA

A WELL-KNOWN musician was deploring in my presence the other day the inroads the cinema was making upon the musical profession. He had just heard, he said, that a cathedral organist had been lured away to play at a cinema; "bribed" was the word he used, "bribed" by more money. The depth of moral degradation suggested by that word "bribed" is awful, and yet as I sat carefully searching my conscience I found nothing but a desire that someone would attempt to bribe me.

Why, I asked, should it be more corrupting to play a Bach Prelude and Fugue in a cinema than in a cathedral? Let us examine the problem in an impartial spirit! Purely as musician, what matters is the quality of the playing. An organist might well refuse to play a Bach Prelude and Fugue on a bad organ, or in a hall with bad acoustics. As a pure musician that is as far as he could go. An organist with a high sense of moral uplift might demand an attentive audience. If you desire to improve people by sound you must, of course, first see that they listen. But there is no way of making people listen. The musician who will not play until he has absolute silence, demands silence so that those who want to listen may do so undisturbed. But I do not think it is the musician's business to obtain silence. I think it concerns those who want to listen to see that they are not disturbed. The " hush ! ", if required, should come from them, not from the performer. The organist who, when playing the organ, has any mission other than playing as well as he possibly can, is a bad organist, though he may be a good father and an excellent architect. But assuming that in instrument, acoustics and audience the cathedral and the cinema are equally well served, how far is the musician to allow other considerations to influence him ? For example, suppose he is a man of taste, and the cinema building is an offence to his eye, should he say : " I refuse to play in your loathsome scaffolding of gilt and white paint ; give me a decent building and I'll play in it ? " Should he then say : " I cannot play good music, and thus attract people, to your filthy film-plays " ? Once he begins to think of anything but his music, where is he going to stop ? Obviously, as a man and a citizen, all sorts of considerations should weigh with him, and the nearer the ideal citizen he is, the more of them there should be for him ; but in practice compromise is inevitable, and one can only say that while a man is acting from feeling, and not from any theoretic principles, his action will be the right action for him. If he is indifferent to the architecture of the building in which he plays, and if he is indifferent to the thousands of feet of meaningless filmed gesticulation which are unrolled daily before millions of two-legged mammals, let him play.

It is possible to get perturbed and excited at such indifference when one definitely believes, as I believe, that the cinema is a drug which is rapidly taking the place of gin and whisky as a dope for the masses, but one may work oneself up into a state of great excitement, and then be met with the calm statement from someone that he habitually goes to the cinema for an hour's rest in a comfortable seat—the difference in the environment giving just that slight stimulation necessary to repose that one gets, for example, when one sleeps in a different house. And, after all, what is wrong with dope? Is not everything dope? It is so very dangerous to dogmatise about the badness of anything that there is little fear of the cinema being boycotted even by people who genuinely believe that it is making good music and good drama more difficult to obtain.

I was told of a certain seaside town which, with some difficulty, had supported an orchestra. For years this orchestra flourished on a small annual loss. Presently, however, the loss grew greater and greater, the reason being that the town was getting better and better supplied with amusements, so that, whereas once upon a time if you wanted to go anywhere in the evening there was only the orchestral concert to go to, now there were half-a-dozen large, comfortable cinemas. The musicians abused the cinemas, but they ought to have abused the people. They had enjoyed a sham audience for years; now they were getting their real public—the people who went not because there was nowhere else to go but because they wanted music. To-day they fear that the town may lose its orchestra altogether. Last year it would have gone had it not been for the support of two Labour members on its Town Council. This year the loss will probably be greater. What ought to be the attitude of the Council? If I were a member I should get up and say : " Gentlemen, the fact that there is a large loss on the municipal orchestra —granted that the orchestra is a good one and that it plays good music—is the best possible proof of its value and the need for its retention. The Town Council is not a commercial business, and if the orchestra were making a profit, our connection with it would not only be superfluous but highly immoral. We exist to give people something a little bit too good for them—better drains, better housing, better music than they want—so that they may learn to like it and so raise their standard of life. We compel them to pay for these luxuries out of the rates. Naturally, they would prefer to pay no rates and live in undisturbed squalor. If we succumb to this wholly base desire then, as a Town Council, we are a complete farce."

My musical friend is so alarmed at the possibility of Bournemouth losing its municipal orchestra that he wants to set in motion a violent propaganda against cinemas. I think he is right to this extent, that no man should spend sixpence on the cinema who has got sense enough to spend it better. It is not merely a question of intelligence and good taste; it is a question of character. An incredible slackness prevents most of us from getting what we want. Rather than accumulate sixpences and go to the theatre or to a symphony concert, rather than start early and go a train or 'bus journey to the "Old Vic," the average man who is sufficiently alive to be dissatisfied with film photographs, drops grumbling into the nearest picture house because it is so convenient. After all, it requires tremendous tenacity to hunt down what you want in face of the hundreds of thousands who do not want it and who cannot see why you should. But unless every one of us exercises this discrimination, the best work is bound to suffer. If the more critical abandon their standards in practice, it is useless their supporting them in theory. This runs all through life. It is as true dealing with the grocer as it is dealing with concerts. The woman who is too slack to complain if the butter falls off in quality is not only letting down all the others who get their butter from the same place, but she is definitely making it more difficult to obtain good butter and is injuring those who produce it. Only by the constant exercise of everybody's taste and judgment can the better article hold its own and gradually usurp the place of the inferior. I knew a man who regularly bought seats to give away when Brahms's symphonies were played, and always kept away numbers of musical people by inviting them to a party when Tchaikovsky filled the bill. Such men, if they have a sense of humour, are the salt of the earth. I say " if they have a sense of humour," because crude propaganda always defeats itself. After listening for two solid hours to my musical friend's abuse of the cinema, I was filled on his departure with an intense desire to go to one. And I have not been inside a film palace for twelve months ! As for the music that is performed in these places, I hear with complete indifference that a movement from the " Moonlight Sonata " accompanies the love-scene between Mary and Reginald in *How He Won her—a Six-Reel Drama with a Real Human Interest*. Some might think it degradation, but you cannot degrade Beethoven, who would have extended his sympathy to all lovers, however dull and imperfect. But how anyone who has listened to the music of Beethoven or read *Romeo and Juliet* or the poetry of John Donne can sit out these six-reel dramas is simply beyond me. I can only conclude that Beethoven, Shakespeare and Donne never meant anything to them, and that education, as I have long suspected, is not what it is supposed to be. But, of course, like my other friend, they may go to the six-reel dramas to avoid something even less pleasant, or to sleep. I am sure the authors of the six-reel dramas do not mind, but what about our cathedral organist? Well, hasn't he been accustomed to it too?

THE PLACE OF EMOTION IN MUSIC

MR. ROBERT LYND, referring to my advocacy of " unadulterated music " in *Music and Life*, once wrote : " The truth of the matter is, of course, that love like Dante's or hatred of tyranny such as Shelley's is an expression of the spirit just as much as their poetry is . . . to treat love and the passion for liberty in an artist as ' physical and accidental like Carlyle's dyspepsia ' is to pretend that a river has nothing to do with the landscape that it enriches and that enriches it in turn."

Now, I agree with this, although we ought all to beware of sentences which begin " the truth of the matter is." With a modesty which, as you will soon see, is only momentary, I declare that I do not know what the truth of the matter is, but what I said and what I still believe to be part of the truth is that neither hatred of tyranny nor love constitute great music or great poetry. Would Mr. Lynd say that no one but Shelley had ever hated tyranny, or that no one but Dante—and a few other poets—had ever loved ? Unless he says that, then it must be admitted that the poetry of Shelley and Dante is something

275

more than hatred and love. But Mr. Lynd will then no doubt add that other men may have loved and hated, but that Dante and Shelley *expressed* that love and that hatred, which the rest were unable to do. Would he have us believe that the *expression* of " love " or the *expression* of " hatred " can constitute great poetry ?

I believe that what Mr. Lynd is doing when he talks about " love " and " hatred " is simply this : he is abstracting certain qualities from the poetry of Dante and Shelley and making these abstractions the actual begetters of the wholes from which they were taken. He finds these certain qualities in other human beings who were not poets, and he then says : " Behold ! these qualities or ' emotions ' are the authors of all art—music, painting and poetry ; but somehow— we none of us understand why—they produce this art only through the medium of certain gifted individuals." Now surely this is very mysterious ? Why " gifted " ? In what exactly does this giftedness consist ? Well, of course, much has been written elaborating, dividing and subdividing this giftedness—sense of rhythm, of colour, richness of vocabulary, power of imagery ; these are but a few out of hundreds—yet what is this classification but a fresh catalogue of qualities found in the works of art under examination ? I maintain that Mr. Lynd might just as well extract from a poem sense of rhythm, or any other quality, and elevate that to the position of "onlie begetter," as raise to that supremacy the passion of love or of hatred or any other passion. I contend that where you have a poem or a musical composition of which you can say this is the expression of such and such an emotion, you are *ipso facto* dealing with an inferior work of art. You are, in fact, contemplating a work of utility, an intellectual or emotional counter.

As an extreme example, supposing I am in a theatre and I am suddenly seized with panic and shout " Fire ! " That scream " Fire ! " is an expression of my emotion, it satisfies Mr. Lynd and the emotionalists' definition of art because it produces a strong emotional reaction in those who hear it. In fact, it is indistinguishable from a Beethoven Sonata—if a work of art is the successful expression through words, or some other medium, of emotion. But not only is my cry " Fire ! " indistinguishable in its nature from a Beethoven Sonata—if we consider art as the expression of emotion—it is also a stronger work of art than any Beethoven Sonata, since it expresses and calls forth a stronger emotion.

Now here is where the emotionalists think they have us. They interpose with " Ah ! but Beethoven expresses a higher emotion ; that is where the difference lies ! " Very well ; but what is the emotion that Beethoven's Sonata Opus III expresses ? Let them tell us, and we will see if we can judge whether it is " higher " or " lower " than my panic when I cry " Fire ! " or than the emotion expressed in a mother's scream when her child is run over by an L.C.C. tram ? Unfortunately there is no man living who can tell us ! Many writers of programme notes may make the attempt, but if they were successful what would be the point of hearing the Sonata ?

Where the emotionalists are misled is in thinking that Croce and those who, like myself, declare that art is not the expression of emotion, deny any place to emotion in the life of the artist. It would be as untrue to say that art is the expression of personal experience as to say that art is the expression of emotion—for obviously every human being is a reservoir of past experience stretching infinitely backwards beyond the human race itself—but an artist's capacity for human emotions is interwoven with his whole vitality. The greater the artist the greater his capacity for emotion ; but to say the greater the capacity for emotion the greater the artist is only true given that he *is* an artist, just as it is true to say that the greater the chord the greater the circle of which it is a part, *provided there is a circle*. We may, however, have no circle but only a chord of a circle. Art is the circle—*i.e.* " feeling that has become all brilliant representation " ; emotion is only the chord.

It is the chief task of the critic to put his finger upon the literary or musical products of his time and to say : Here is—or is not—a work of art.

If he can say of any work : this is the expression of such and such an emotion or idea, and that is a fairly adequate description of it—then he is not dealing with a genuine work of art at all.

The genuine work of art gives us an æsthetic pleasure which is unique and which is not to be translated into any particular emotion or thought. The inferior artist is always falling back on such tricks as calling " Fire ! "—appeals to emotions which are comparatively easy to arouse, or, in the case of the intelligentsia, to our intellectual theories. Good examples of the former are to be found in Tchaikovsky's music and in Böcklin's pictures. Excellent examples of the latter are to be found in the music of all modern composers.

But primitive man's perception of the mere difference between a musical sound and a noise was also æsthetic. It was æsthetic in the sense that it was the foundation of all future musical perception. We see how difficult it is to assign an exact meaning to any word ! At what point in the development of the human mind does the word " æsthetic " become necessary ? It arises when intellectual perception has become so highly developed that it takes on a new character. But there is no definite line of demarcation to be drawn ; innumerable intellectual perceptions shade into and colour your æsthetic. The most abstract art is full of emotional echoes. They are the load and the inheritance of past perceptions. Any living musician, given half a Mozart melody, can finish it—not from a particular memory of that air, but from the general musical memory of the human race. I have made up thousands of variations on themes by Mozart, Beethoven and Brahms in my bath and in railway carriages. But, although they have often been as good as variations by the composers themselves, they have absolutely no value because they are mere race-memory. They have no æsthetic significance; they can only stir emotions in the memory. I have discovered that this is what I have meant when I have criticised music adversely as being too "emotional." What it amounts to is that such music is not original enough. *When a song, a poem, or a painting has real æsthetic significance, we cannot recognise the emotion it awakes in us because that emotion is new, it is something we have not experienced before.*

The great mass of literature, music and painting produced annually has no æsthetic value at all. That is to say, it has no value. Here I am dealing in absolutes for the sake of effect. In practice, this annual production is perhaps of varying value, for even the finest work has echoes. There is nothing absolutely new, yet the difference between the most original art and the average "artistic" production is so great that to pronounce them absolutely different is, for the average person, less misleading than to say merely that they differ.

We are up against one difficulty, and it is this: how is one to determine the relative value of works of art if, as Croce seems to think, all genuine works of art are of equal æsthetic value, each being unique ? Are the wonderful drawings of reindeer by some palæolithic cave-man of equal æsthetic value to the Beethoven Sonata Opus III ? Considered purely æsthetically according to Croce, they are. But, says Croce, there is another mode of classification, and it is called *History*. True criticism of art is historical " not because, like pseudo-history, it deals with the externals of art, but because, after having availed itself of historical data for imaginative reproduction (and till then it is not history), when imaginative reproduction has been obtained it becomes history." It is also philosophical, and one work of art may be of more philosophical importance than another. So we may say Beethoven's music is more " important " than Mozart's, although, purely æsthetically, they are equal. Here we run up against a disastrous snag which Croce has not seen but which wrecks his theory. We can admit that Beethoven's music is more important than Mozart's from our new point of view without damage to the validity of our æsthetic criticism, provided we feel that æsthetically they are equal ; but what if we think that in Mozart the feeling has " become all brilliant representation," while in Beethoven it has not ? In other words, what if Mozart's music is a work of art, but Beethoven's is not ? Where are we now ? This is what all philosophic criticism does to us. It carries us forward at a breakneck speed, illuminating the path before us with a dazzling searchlight *which suddenly goes out*. The reason is always that philosophy deals with the ideal. The work of art, as Croce imagines it, has never existed. There is no perfect work of art, none in which the feeling has all become image. Yet what Croce says remains true; but the whole truth has not yet made its concrete appearance on this earth, and never will.

WHAT IS GOOD MUSIC?

MUSIC has always been the great stumbling-block to critics in their generalisations about æsthetics. In literature we have seen a revulsion from the cry of the eighteen-nineties, "Art for art's sake," which in its turn was a revulsion from the superficial moralising of Ruskin. To Ruskin Gothic architecture was morally virtuous, and that was why it was good architecture. It was designed and built by honest workmen, workmen who lived virtuous lives, did not know the meaning of divorce, and who consequently never botched or scamped a job. With the Renaissance men became wicked, selfish, self-conscious, and irreligious. Consequently they were charlatans, and their work was meretricious—clever perhaps, but insincere. This delightfully simple but ingenious theory was taken to the hearts of the English people. It was so easy to understand, for one thing; and for another it was so flattering to everybody. For the wicked never mind being thought wicked if it is allowed that they are clever; and as for the good—well, they could be as dull and stupid as they liked, but nevertheless they could not be incompetent, because it was axiomatic in the Ruskinian æsthetics that the good produced good work.

Ruskin was the most muddle-headed genius the world has ever produced. It is obvious to the merest schoolboy that you may be good to your mother—*i.e.* kind and considerate—without being a good wicket-keeper, or vice-versa. In other words, that there are thousands of varieties of " good," and that the possession of one good does not necessarily put you in possession of all the others. Now, it is inconceivable that Ruskin should not have been able to see this. Why, then, did he persistently, wilfully, close his eyes to it, with the result that he filled London with bad imitation Gothic buildings, and that he praised the works of painters far inferior to Whistler in the most extravagant terms, while describing Whistler as " flinging a pot of paint in the face of the public " ? Was Ruskin an inspired lunatic, or was there some truth buried beneath the absurdities of his attitude—some general idea whose value was so great as to outweigh all the smaller errors of judgment in its application ?

This is a question that has got to be faced by music critics as well as by the critics of all the other arts ; and for my part I have no hesitation in saying that, while no one dislikes more than I do Ruskin's insufferable priggishness and his too superficial and conventional conception of " goodness," yet I am forced to admit that I think Ruskin was on the right track. The followers of

Wilde and Whistler, the "art for art's sake" theorists, are in a *cul-de-sac*. They have got hold of a truth, but it is not all the truth. Ruskin had got hold of a much more obscure and difficult truth. To say that he had "got hold of it" is a euphemism : he really only had got a very dim glimpse of it, but it is a bigger, more comprehensive generalisation than the "art for art's sake" truth, and it enables us to range works of art in a more rational and orderly manner.

The "art for art's sake" theorists are forced by their theory to judge works of art solely by some technical standard. They have no other "system of co-ordinates" to which they can refer them. In fact, by their formula everything becomes a work of art that is not done for money or for any other useful purpose. And they have no method by which they can tell whether it is well done, because technique is an individual thing. There cannot be a technique that is absolutely "it" and good for everybody, for that would introduce an absolute standard outside art by reference to which works of art were good or bad. In this dilemma we find that what happens is that in every age a certain kind of technique becomes fashionable, and the "art for art's sake" champions judge the goodness and badness of contemporary works of art by reference to this fashionable technique. In music the present generation has witnessed no less than four fashions—the Strauss, the Debussy, the Neo-Russian, and the Folk-Song

fashions. During each of these crazes good music
—*i.e.* music that was modern, original, and worth
bothering about—was music that conformed to
the fashionable prototype of the moment; the
rest was rubbish.

Now, Ruskin was quite right when he perceived,
however confusedly, that this habit was all wrong.
It is wrong because it is formless, because it leaves
art without any organisation; and he strove to
give it an organic unity by introducing the
touchstone of moral goodness. Unfortunately
" moral goodness " meant to Ruskin something
far too limited. Ruskin lived during the middle
of the nineteenth century, when England was
still in the grip of Puritanical measles. The
whole country had a sort of moral small-pox.
" Goodness " was narrowed down—was, in fact,
whittled away to a merely negative denial of life.
It was obviously impossible to apply this nineteenth-century test of " moral goodness " to
works of art, because there were no works of art
which were small enough, dead enough, anæmic
enough to be squeezed into so limited a conception.
All the great artistic works of the world were
upon the Puritanical Index; all that was left were
a few hymns.

Now that we have deepened and vivified our
conception of goodness, it may be possible to try
to reapply Ruskin's standard—the standard he
was instinctively aiming at. Men and women get

their perceptions of goodness from life and from works of art. Works of art provide us with a standard of reference which is not technical, not " artistic," but concrete and pure and universal. By " life " I mean our inner life. There is no life outside us except in works of art ; that is why art is so immensely the most important of all human products. What is called " life " by many people is merely material mechanism without any significance. Significance only exists in our own spirit and in works of art in which we touch the spirit of others.

Significance is spiritual, not mechanical. "Goodness " is the measure of the spiritual life. This is the profound truth which Ruskin was aiming at. Art is good according to the fullness in which it expresses spiritual life. Here we have a criterion to apply to all art, including music. But it is a criterion that cannot be applied like a foot-rule. It is not a fool-proof gadget which anybody can use. Only those whose spiritual intuition has grasped the beauty of great works of art possess a core of consciousness to which they can refer new works of art. Now, what I want to say is this—that in music there are two composers whose work towers immensely above the work of most other musicians. Those two are Mozart and Beethoven. Neither Mozart nor Beethoven make his strongest appeal straightway. I well remember when I was a student, about ten years ago, that

I thought Mozart childish and thin. Strauss, Scriabin, and Tchaikovsky seemed to me immeasurably greater. They thrilled me and swept me off my feet; while Mozart left me cold. Now I listen to their works with a chilly, disillusioned mind. I see through all those gentlemen and their corybantic ravings. They no longer can raise a hair upon my head, or stir a muscle in my body—but Mozart! If ever there was a divine spirit born into this world it was Wolfgang Amadeus Mozart. I would ask the reader to get down the A Major Pianoforte Concerto composed in 1786 (when Mozart was thirty years old) and play the first movement slowly through. Then let him play the following slow movement, and when he has finished playing those two movements, he will, if he has any sensibility of soul, know what real goodness is. By the side of that exquisite spiritual beauty the lachrymose howlings of Tchaikovsky and the sensuous orgies of Scriabin seem empty and meaningless. The same is true of Beethoven, who, however, rarely attained the purity of style of Mozart. Yet Mozart was "inordinately fond of punch." In his later years—he died at the early age of thirty-five, harassed and impoverished, and was buried in a pauper's grave—he led a hectic, dissipated life. Beethoven often behaved abominably to his friends, and described his publishers as "hell-hounds who lick and gnaw my brains"; he was normally immoral, and there was not a year in his life when he was not in love with somebody. Yet these two men were spiritually two of the greatest men who have ever been born into this world. So it is obvious that the Puritanical idea of goodness is inadequate.

MUSIC AND MR. H. G. WELLS

AS I sat in the Queen's Hall one afternoon
and listened to M. Maurice Ravel (most
celebrated of living French composers)
conducting his own suite, *Ma Mère l'Oye*, and
then to Sir Henry Wood conducting Schubert's
last Symphony—the one in C always called
No. 7, written in 1828, but unknown until
discovered by Schumann in manuscript in Vienna
in 1838—I suddenly asked myself, "What is the
value of music?" Naturally, it will be assumed
that I have asked myself this question before, but
each time one asks a question the answer is
slightly different, and what was the answer
now?

Then it suddenly occurred to me that I could
not remember any reference to music in Mr. H. G.
Wells' renowned world history. Mr. Wells brings
" an inexhaustible curiosity," a " passion for
knowledge and health," " a zeal for truth "—I
quote from imaginary reviews !—to the survey of
the earth and all that has ever been on it, and he
cannot even find any sign of the existence of this
stuff we call music. Strange ! Almost incom-

prehensible ! I looked around me. Upwards of sixty strong, full-grown men were furiously scraping wooden machines with rods or blowing hard down brass tubes ; Sir Henry Wood, *Knight*, was busy at it, cutting the air into rhythmical patterns with a stick ; thousands of men and women filled the auditorium with their silence. The past, with its departed thousands playing and listening, also surged about me. " All fools," I thought ; " in the history of the world, in *The Outline of History*, you do not exist." I began to think my memory must be deceiving me. So, when I returned home, still troubled by that unanswered question, wondering indeed whether the question had any meaning—if, as it seemed, music and musicians, the Queen's Hall, M. Maurice Ravel, Sir Henry Wood, all were mere emanations of my disordered brain and had no real existence !—I procured and searched the index of *The Outline of History*. What did I find ? *Music ?* No ! the word " music " does not appear in the index, but, instead, there is something else, some other entry, startling in its significance : *Musical Instruments*, 57. Not " music," but " musical instruments " ! Then I looked up the letter B to find Beethoven. In the history of man Beethoven should be of some importance. No Beethoven ! And no Bach, no Mozart, no Wagner, but—" musical instruments " ! Perhaps the significance of this escapes you as it first escaped me. You are so sure that music has a value, and a considerable value. Well, I must put alongside this dismissal of music the following statement taken from the same pen in a recent article on the ten most important books :

> "The reader will remark that I have glanced at Homer and the *Rig Veda* only to dismiss them, and that Shakespeare and Goethe, Euripides and Virgil, and so forth, are not even named. But I was not asked for the most beautiful or the most perfect or the most moving books ; I was asked for the most important. I was thinking not of delights, but powers. And just as I declined to think of Shakespeare, that most lovable, humorous, melodious, and understanding man, as one of the six greatest men, so do I refuse to consider his plays, or any one of his plays, as of supreme importance in human affairs. Had there never been a Shakespeare the world would have been much what it is to-day, some of us would have lacked a dear friend, and the forcing-houses of ' refinement ' would have had one tedious cant the less."

As one reads that incredible drivel, one wonders whether words have now any meaning at all for the writer of it. He was not asked for the " most beautiful," the " most perfect," or the " most moving," but the " most important," the most powerful. Well! well! but is there no power in the " beautiful," the " perfect," the " moving " ? If there is no power in our emotions, where is " power " ? In dry, dead accumulations of fact ? In statistics ? In machines without purpose or feeling ? In " musical instruments," but not in " music " ? What is this but the latest and most childish materialism ? Surely, what chiefly differentiates man from other animals, as well as from plants and stones, are his feelings. It is in the development of man's sensibility, of man's spirituality, that all Mr. Wells' best hopes lie, and in this development it is the Homers, the Shakespeares, the Virgils, the Goethes, the Bachs and the Beethovens of the world that have played the greatest part. They have influenced men's desires, they have helped them to *want* what they have not yet got, and without that impelling spiritual emotion, the most wonderful of machines, the most highly organised social system would be an idiotic terror.

When one criticises music, one does not do so by counting the number of the instruments in the band or measuring the amount of noise made. You do not know a good violinist by the number of strings on his fiddle or the number of fingers on his hand, nor even by his agility or cleverness. The ultimate test is an æsthetic, a spiritual test. That is the most important, the greatest " power."

When music sinks to the level of technics, that is a sure sign of its degeneration, and it is by a higher standard that mankind judges Schubert's Symphony in C Major to be of greater value than M. Ravel's " Mother Goose " suite.

It is curious to find virulent in Mr. Wells the bad nineteenth-century scientific materialism. Even in the nineteenth century, however, the best scientific minds were free from it. You would never find such superficiality in a really great artist or scientist. Without the desire for under-standing there could have been no science. It is desire that precedes knowledge, and I strongly believe that the greatest scientists, like the greatest artists, seek the same reality, although it may be shown to us in a different form. I quote the words of a mathematician, Mr. J. W. N. Sullivan, from a recent book : " The matter of the highest art, like that of true science, is reality, and the measure in which science falls short as art is the measure in which it is incomplete as science."

To many people, art means " musical instru-ments," and science means telephones, aeroplanes and wireless broadcasting. They need to be educated to a deeper understanding of life. But they will not be helped by the superficial notions of the cheap panacea-monger, and it is regrettable to find one of the greatest " powers " (measured quantitatively) of our age spoon-feeding a large uneducated English public in *John o' London's*

Weekly with such ignorant clap-trap as I have quoted from Mr. Wells. If that is a typical example of educating the people in science, literature and history, the less of this " education " they have the better.

AN EXPLANATION

A LETTER appeared in *The Times* in February 1924 under the signatures of Sir Alexander Mackenzie, the retiring Principal of the Royal Academy of Music, and of Sir Hugh Allen, the Director of the Royal College of Music, on the proposed visit of the Vienna State Opera Company to Covent Garden the following May. The letter began by confessing the writers' reluctance to join in the controversy which the proposed visit had incited—but why this reluctance? If the proposed visit of a foreign State Musical Organisation to this country is the subject of a controversy, who could take part in such a controversy more appropriately than the heads of the two leading official musical organisations of this country? The real reason for Sir Hugh Allen's and Sir Alexander Mackenzie's "reluctance," however, is not far to seek. It appears immediately in the second sentence of their joint letter, which reads:

> "In common with many others we should like to hear the performances of this company, but we feel that no time could be less appropriate than that which is to be dedicated to the assembling at a great exhibition

of all the best this Empire can produce for
the delight and instruction of probably the
greatest number of British subjects ever
brought together."

The " reluctance " of our two chief musical
academicians is, therefore, an admission that as
musicians they recognise that they have no
business to oppose the visit of a body of foreign
musicians. As British subjects, however, duty
compels them to speak, but only " with considerable reluctance." This is as it should be.
I appreciate the dilemma with which these
gentlemen are faced. How can they reconcile
their duty as musicians with their duty as
Britishers ! It is an unfortunate situation, and
they have my deepest sympathy. With the ruling
class of the last hundred years, and with that
large, dull, apathetic region known to sociological
cosmographers as the " middle classes," who have
been jointly responsible for putting these two
distinguished Britishers in such an unfortunate
position, I have, however, no sympathy at all.

Making the best of a bad job, Sir Hugh and
Sir Alexander proceed to a eulogy of the British
National Opera Company :

" In the B.N.O.C. we have an organisation, young in years, strong in personnel,
brilliant in promise—a real home-grown
product."

297

I admire this statement, its careful sense of proportion, its desire for accuracy, its avoidance of any exaggerations of the B.N.O.C.'s *perform-ance*, but with that compensating, almost delirious, "brilliant in promise." Ah, Sir Hugh Allen! Oh, Sir Alexander Mackenzie! What a phrase—"brilliant in promise"! Let me not belittle the B.N.O.C. Considering the state of public culture they have done wonders. I have heard them give enjoyable performances of immensely difficult works. They possess singers and con-ductors of talent. They have put up a fight, and although they have not done exceedingly or outstandingly well they have done well. During this last season I had the pleasure of hearing an atrocious performance of *The Magic Flute* under Mr. Julius Harrison. Insufficient rehearsal would account for the lack of finish, the rough crudity of the singing and playing, but it was hardly an excuse for Mr. Julius Harrison's rendering of the overture.

It ought to have been impossible for Mr. Harrison to have allowed the orchestra to give such a dull, slovenly performance. But does Mr. Harrison understand *The Magic Flute?* Where was Mozart's demoniacal clang? Cer-tainly not where it should have been in the Queen of the Night's famous aria. This should be sung with diabolic verve. It is satanic music, a magical incantation, and it knocks flat all the mock magicians of music. It is sad to hear a conductor fail in his duty to a composer. He should always have in his mind as he mounts his rostrum that he has a revelation to make. Here, again, my sympathy is stirred. To whom is Mr. Julius Harrison to make his revelation? To Clapham, Balham, Muswell Hill, Highgate, Wimbledon and Putney! No, Mr. Harrison, fortunately it is not to these self-satisfied bourgeois masses that you have to make your revelation, but to an isolated being here or there in that vast auditorium who can hear and understand—although you may have done something to the others also. To Mr. Harrison's credit may be put a quite enjoyable performance of *Tristan and Isolde*. But there is no need to examine the B.N.O.C.'s productions in detail. It is enough to say that no one has even suggested that the B.N.O.C. should give an exchange season in Vienna.

That the conductor, the executive musician, has a revelation to make, that it is the sole reason of his being, is not to be doubted. We have lately been enjoying the visit to London of Herr Wilhelm Furtwängler, the successor of Arthur Nikisch at Leipzig. Herr Furtwängler conducted at the last Philharmonic Society's concert a programme of Handel, Strauss and Brahms. His conducting of Strauss's *Don Juan* was a revelation of its romantic and sentimental beauty. The Handel (Concerto Grosso in D Minor for Strings) was a revelation of a different sort, it was a revelation of the coarseness and perfunctory inexpressiveness of the playing of this type of music by our average English conductor. The Brahms was no revelation. Here, for the first time, I thought Herr Furtwängler lost sight of the whole in its parts. At the following London Symphony Concert, however, I had a real revelation. I heard for the first time in my life a completely satisfactory interpretation of Beethoven's C Minor Symphony. I say interpretation, not performance, for the orchestral playing was by no means perfect. I have heard this symphony dozens of times, as every musical amateur has. I thought I knew all about it, and I have even had the audacity to say that the last movement was a proof that Beethoven could not build up a really satisfactory orchestral climax. Well, after hearing Herr Furtwängler's rendering I take that back. I eat my own words. Beethoven, as might have been expected, knew better than I what he was doing. I should have been able to understand, but I didn't thoroughly understand until Herr Furtwängler showed me. His interpretation was in no way superficially startling. He took no liberties with the tempi, he gave a perfectly straightforward performance, but a performance in which I heard lots of things that I had never heard before. The chief difference between this and other renderings I have heard was in the phrasing of the strings and the wood-wind. I have often heard renderings of this symphony which made me feel how dramatic and over-whelming were its ideas, but I never before heard one that made me feel how perfect was its workmanship. Here, then, is a complete justifi-cation of Herr Furtwängler, and it provides us with the obvious reason for welcoming the visits of foreign artists. We do not know everything. We do not even know how little we know, and if we keep strictly to ourselves we shall never know. I feel that a visit from the Vienna State Opera Company is a national need. I feel that however deplorable it may be that we have not got a State Opera Company at all, and however politic it might be to attempt to disguise our beggary behind the B.N.O.C., we had far better expose ourselves to the world's ridicule during the British Empire Exhibition. The British Empire Exhibition finds us without a National Opera Company, without a National Theatre, without Shakespeare, without drama and without music. Instead, we have the Stadium and the echoes of the Football Association Cup-ties or Cup-finals. It is a very pretty phenomenon. I will present my readers with another to keep it company. Every Saturday night Covent Garden Opera House is *sold out* for performances of *La Bohème* or *Madame Butterfly*. The house is probably never more than half-full for *The Valkyrie*, *Siegfried*, *Tristan and Isolde* and *The Magic Flute*. The management does not even attempt to give *Rhinegold* and *The Twilight of the Gods*. It has publicly stated that the Russian operas do not pay. Why cannot the B.N.O.C. give the *Ring* in its entirety as its composer intended it to be given? Why cannot it give those magnificent works *Boris Godounov, Coq d'Or, Khovantchina?* Why cannot it give *Pelléas and Mélisande* and *Don Giovanni?* Because the London public only goes to the opera on a Saturday night. It goes out once a week, and it does not care where it goes. I stood one Saturday night in February 1924 and watched the suburbs rolling up to Covent Garden in their Standards, Sunbeams, Rovers, Beans, Morris-Cowleys, Morris-Oxfords, Wolseleys and all the other kinds of motor-cars for the middle-classes, and as I looked at them I understood why we have no National Opera, no National Theatre, no drama, no music.

DEMOCRACY AND THE ARTS

THE majority of artists in this country view the accession of a Labour Government to office with a mingling of joy and misgiving. The true artist—and here is a useful touchstone to help to discern him—has no illusions as to the value of the aristocratic or plutocratic patron. The aristocratic patron as an individual he sees to be generally no more intelligent, no more honourable, than the average working man. Nor is he less limited, although his limitations are different. Nor has he had, until recently, a tradition differing in essentials. In literature the chief English classics, the Bible and Shakespeare, were as familiar to the average labourer as to the average landlord. In architecture our Gothic, Tudor and Georgian masterpieces were at least as fully appreciated by the average workman, who helped to build them, as by the average Norman prize-fighter or commercial tout who amassed the wealth to pay for them and founded the families to live in them. But the artist does not believe that there is more virtue in one class than another. He tries to see things as they are. He does not put the bricklayer above the Norman prize-fighter; he does not believe that :

" Kind hearts are more than coronets,
And simple faith than Norman blood."

303

He does not even think they are incompatibles; in fact, the two phrases, "kind hearts" and "Norman blood," he finds so vague and meaningless that he can do nothing with them, he cannot even use them in a satire.

To-day he has advanced so far that he only completely and utterly believes in the artist. But lest this should seem just another form of vanity he will admit that the perfect artist has never existed. A man is only an artist in so far as he sees things as they really are. It is the devotion of a man's whole powers to this heroic attempt that makes a man an artist—whether he expresses his conclusions in music, painting, sculpture, literature or any other medium. If anyone should call this "realism" he is completely silly.

When the artist contemplates the society in which he lives he sees that the enjoyment of wealth and leisure—like the suffering of poverty and misfortune—has on the majority of men both a refining and a debasing effect. No one has yet attempted to analyse this process, although it certainly is a problem to be studied before many years pass; but stated in that way it is not a problem for the artist. He feels instinctively, however, that he is strongly desirous of increasing wealth and leisure for an ever higher proportion of society. Not only does he want wealth and leisure, but, most emphatically, luxury. In this desire he finds himself at one with the general feeling of mankind, for in spite of the sporadic

304

and persistent outbursts of puritanism—which, like the recurring epidemics of influenza, are not inexplicable—the desire for luxury is universal in men. It is no good any communistic group thinking it can permanently dominate this desire. The utmost it can do is to add a new luxury to the list—the luxury of haircloth in a world of *crêpe-de-Chine*.

But in a survey of civilisation the artist is faced with a phenomenon which staggers him. He sees that while in no generation has the best been popular, nevertheless, the best only has survived from generation to generation. The complete neglect of Shelley by an age which bought hundreds of thousands of copies of Mr. Martin Tupper is the sort of example (among hundreds) which is usually brought forward, but I will content myself with referring to a more recent event, namely, the sneers in the popular Press by " Mr. Gossip," directed against Dr. Robert Bridges, on his visit in 1924 to America. Dr. Bridges is known by those who have troubled to read his work as a distinguished poet. There is a poem by him entitled *London Snow* which is likely to outlive the total production of many of the day's famous authors. The name of Robert Bridges is unknown to all but a tiny group. What a mystery it is that Dr. Bridges and not some inferior but far more popular writer is Poet Laureate ! Will such good fortune be possible under a Labour Government, or shall we get as Poet Laureate the author of some trashy verbiage which he has astutely entitled *Ode to Democracy, God and the People*, or more adroitly still, *Revolution?* It may be truly said that, while there have been greater Poet Laureates than Dr. Robert Bridges, his beneficial influence on our language has been second to none. The only justification, the only meaning of such an office as Poet Laureate is to put into the hands of the right man the job of preventing a fall in the standard of writing. This Dr. Bridges, with his well-known " Society of Pure English," has done. It is the reason of being of all " official " artists. Sir Hugh Allen, of the Royal College of Music, and Sir Alexander Mackenzie, of the Royal Academy of Music, are not expected to produce great composers. Only God can produce *them*, but these gentlemen are expected to see that the standard of musicianship does not fall. Some of us even expect them to raise it ; that is why we cannot understand how, as musicians, Sir Hugh Allen and Sir Alexander Mackenzie can oppose the visit to this country of foreign musicians from whom we may all learn something.

But I confess I am not afraid of what English Labour Governments will do and, lest some Russian communist should laugh ironically at this, I add, immediately, because I have too high an opinion of the sound common-sense of this country. The most hopeful event that has happened since the French Revolution is the advent in England of the first constitutional Labour Government in Europe. Beside this the Russian revolution, desirable as it was, is almost insignificant. I call to mind that the vulgar ignorant abuse of Dr. Robert Bridges has been in the anti-Socialist Press and not in *The Daily Herald*. I might refer to the " Old Vic " audiences, but I have no belief or hope in popularity. What is important is the spirit of a party and the character of its leaders. The fact that the tendency of the Labour Party is and will be to take art seriously is immensely stimulating and extremely dangerous. Stimulating because it is essentially right and in harmony with man's deepest instincts; dangerous because of our little knowledge. It may be said that every active furtherance of art by the Labour Party—the gift of a grant towards a National Theatre, the wider encouragement of general artistic and educational enterprise, will be wholly to the good. The Labour Party will support art and artists with deeds where the other parties have damned them with faint and suspicious praise. But any *restrictive* action on the part of a Labour Government, any attempt to censor works of art, any attempt to suppress what may be thought by a respectable citizen to be ignoble, indecent, wicked, immoral, blasphemous or irreligious art, will be fatal and so pernicious as to nullify the best intentions in the world. The ennobling of art must be left to the artists; only they understand that extraordinarily complex and subtle job. The Labour Party must adopt as their guide in these matters Milton, who denounced magnificently the censorship of books. The way to support art and artists is to subsidise what you think good, not to try and suppress what you think bad. And here I may aptly quote from a pamphlet, *British Music*, published at sixpence by H.M. Stationery Office. It is a report of the Adult Education Committee, which included such representative names as Sir Hugh Allen, Sir Henry Hadow, Mr. H. C. Colles (musical critic of *The Times*), Sir Walford Davies, Mr. Geoffrey Shaw and Mr. Hamilton Harty. I will quote two passages :

I. " Sir Hugh Allen informed us that the Bach Choir at Oxford, after seven weeks' study, gave recently an admirable performance of Beethoven's *Mass in D*, which a little time ago would have required a year's work and twenty years ago could not have been attempted. He attributed the improvement in the main to the better teaching in the ' public ' schools.

II. " It is clear, however, that fully adequate performances of many of the greatest operas *cannot be given at a profit*, and that these works will not become a national possession while the matter rests in private hands."

The italics are mine. Let me add that I read

that passage with a shout of joy. If ever there was a monstrous and wicked conception it is the idea that works of art should yield a commercial profit. The one ultimately convincing reason why all artists without exception should welcome the advent of the Labour Party into power is that it is not a victim of this ridiculous delusion. The man who thinks that access to the greatest works of art should be left for private speculators to provide may be thought by some people to be merely an optimistic idiot ; he is something much worse, he is a frivolous fool.

THE *RING*

" I start for England on Friday. Wagner,
who is directing the old London Philharmonic (a post I was obliged to refuse, being
engaged by the other society), is buried
beneath the vituperations of the whole
British Press. He remains calm, for he says
that *in fifty years he will be master of the
musical world.*"

. . . . . .

" Meyerbeer ought to be pleased with the
reception of the *Étoile du Nord* at Covent
Garden. They threw him bouquets, as
though he were a prima donna."—*Extract
of a letter from Hector Berlioz to Auguste
Morel dated June,* 1855.

WAGNER was forty-two in 1855, and
had just completed, in the May of the
previous year, the composition of *Das
Rheingold.* He had already begun *Die Walküre*
and, indeed, wrote some of the instrumentation
during his stay in London, but—

" it only advanced a paltry hundred pages.
I was hindered in this principally by the
circumstance that the sketches from which
I had to work on the instrumentation had

been written down without considering the extent to which a prolonged interruption of my working humour might affect the coherence of the sketch. How often did I sit before those pencilled pages as if they had been unfamiliar hieroglyphics which I was incapable of deciphering. In absolute despair I plunged into Dante, making for the first time a serious effort to read him. The *Inferno*, indeed, became a never-to-be-forgotten reality in that London atmosphere."

Nevertheless, with *Meistersinger* and *Tristan und Isolde* unwritten, and with the *Ring* only just begun, Wagner had a confidence in himself beside which Napoleon's faith in his star was a feeble miscalculation. It is now seventy years since Wagner wrote those words Berlioz quoted, and Wagner has been " master of the musical world " since the opening of Bayreuth in 1876. As far as I can see he is likely to remain so for an indefinite time to come, because I believe that Wagner occupies in the world of music the place held by Shakespeare in English literature, and, as we all know, a Shakespeare is not born every century. I believe—antipathetic as some of Wagner's music is to me, and conscious as I am of his limitations—that we shall never have a greater musical work than the *Ring*. I do not believe we shall never have one as great, but whatever genius there is to come the *Ring* will remain the *Ring*, and as incomparable with what is to follow as it is to-day with all that went before.

A modern literary critic of great intelligence has declared that *Hamlet* is not a perfect work of art and has produced some excellent arguments in support of his opinion. Good arguments can also be brought to show that the *Ring* is not a perfect work of art. Nobody has ever fully understood *Götterdämmerung*, and there is a general agreement that it is intellectually unsatisfactory. I feel that it is intentionally so because Wagner would not be satisfied with a dramatic conclusion to his tetralogy that was not philosophically satisfactory also. Finding himself unable to create a self-contained complete philosophy, finding ultimately that—in spite of Schopenhauer and his own experience of life— he did *not* know, he had to trust wholly to his intuition and his craftsmanship. So in *Götterdämmerung* we find him falling back more completely on his musical virtuosity. *That*, at least, never failed him. A practised writer—especially if he were a dramatist—reading the poem of *Götterdämmerung*, with care could not fail to feel the purposed avoidance of giving any too definite meaning to the dramatic action. It is deliberately, and with extraordinary skill, that Wagner has made *Götterdämmerung* obscure. We may consider that this hides a real weakness. After all, we do expect the artist to know. This

is true of the smallest as of the greatest artists—
those who are decorators or toy-makers and those
whose toys are not dead but alive! But *Götterdämmerung* is not alive, it is an obscurity, not a
mystery, and it is so, I think, because Wagner
went beyond his powers when he attempted
to grapple with the problem of man and the
universe in the manner of a philosopher. It was
primarily a failure of his dramatic genius, for the
dramatist who attempts to put the whole of life
into a drama can do so only by writing a pure
drama—a drama in which all the elements are so
fused that the resulting work is elemental, that
is to say, unique and indivisible. Then it is a
mystery and has an infinity of meanings, but
where there has not been this complete conception, this perfect fusion, you get obscurity.
Wagner did not perfectly assimilate the ideas
with which his extraordinarily eager and active
mind supplied him. He did not wish to create
merely by intuition; he wanted his intellect
to collaborate with his instinct, and in this he was
like all the greatest artists. It is only the minor
artists who are content to work from intuition
or reason alone. Or perhaps it would be truer
to say that in the supreme, the perfect, artist
intuition and reason would be one. But I do
not care for such an abstraction as the perfect
artist. I prefer imperfect artists like Wagner
and Shakespeare. My criticism of Wagner is
that in his greatest and most daring work he

failed to achieve what he set out to do. No
matter how often I hear the *Ring*, I am completely
convinced until I arrive at *Götterdämmerung*.
Dull patches here and there I used to find when
I was first familiar with *Rheingold*, *Walküre* and
Siegfried have one by one disappeared with every
hearing until there are no dull patches, no dull
moments even, in the first three music dramas
of the cycle, and if there ever seem to be, I know
now it is the fault of the singers or the orchestra.
The first three parts of the tetralogy are completely alive. And what a magnificence of life!
No need for me to expatiate on the quality and
variety of this life! Mr. Ernest Newman's
twenty-feet shelf-length of books on Wagner
testifies sufficiently to that. Then we come to
Götterdämmerung, and we find all through the
first act no hint of failure. Then comes the
second act and we are rudely shaken. The whole
architecture, grand and sublime as it seemed,
tumbles about our ears. If in *Götterdämmerung*
Wagner had risen to the height of the matter he
had set himself—and which at that point he had
to attempt—the *Ring* would have been incon-
testably and immeasurably the greatest work
of art ever created by man. But in *Rheingold*,
Walküre and *Siegfried* Wagner had scaled mountains, the highest Alps, one may even say, of
music; then he spread his wings to fly into the
empyrean and fell dismally into the mud—
where, of course, he found excellent company,

for almost all the other musicians of the age were crawling there contentedly. And when I say " mud," what I mean is this. Wagner in the second act of *Götterdämmerung* has become self-conscious. The music is fabricated, uninspired; and it is uninspired, I believe, because in its final stage in the poem of *Götterdämmerung* the *Ring* had ceased to be true to Wagner. *Götterdämmerung* had no meaning to Wagner, and that is why it has no meaning to us; but Wagner took enormous pains to hide its emptiness from himself and from us. The *Ring* rather resembles as a work of art Milton's *Paradise Lost ;* in both there are elements which seem eternally true, their mythological form is a form of life. Milton's Satan is an example. Elsewhere there are passages—those, for instance, in which God and his Son speak in Book VI—in which the mythological form contains no reality, merely an imperfect, irrational and obscure philosophical idea. *Paradise Lost* as a philosophy, as an expression of man and the universe, is as great a failure, is as false and insufficient as *Der Ring des Nibelungen*, but like *Paradise Lost* the *Ring* contains many sublime truths. The point that I am anxious to make is just this, that it is only when uttering these sublime truths, only when he wholly felt that what he was expressing was true (which also means—strange paradox !— only when he was unconscious of what he was saying), that Wagner could write great music.

But I believe Wagner became more conscious that he did not believe what he was saying than Milton ever did, although I have my own conviction that in the deepest sense Milton did not believe what he was saying when he wrote :

> "Effulgence of my glory, Son beloved,
> Son in whose face invisible is beheld
> Visibly, what by Deity I am."

But Milton had a more ingeniously devised, more self-contained, fool-proof mechanism in his mythology than Wagner had, and although his soul could not believe in it, as his own poem proves, yet his intellect could accept it. Wagner, I feel, was intellectually uneasy as well as spiritually faithless in the *Götterdämmerung*, but, possessing a musical virtuosity as great as Milton's verbal virtuosity, he covered up his uneasiness with prodigious signs. But how the music changes when he gets something in which he again believes ! What a change from the artificial paroxysms of so much of Act II to the Trauermarsch of Act III ! But death is always an unfailing stimulus to artistic genius, and in spite of the Trauermarsch and the closing scene, *Götterdämmerung* always leaves me with the feeling that I have been cheated of a sublime experience.

THE END

ol